FORGOTTEN REFUGEES

Two Iraqi Brothers in India

Nandita Haksar

SPEAKING
TIGER

SPEAKING TIGER BOOKS LLP
125A, Ground Floor, Shahpur Jat, near Asiad Village,
New Delhi 110049

First published by Speaking Tiger Books 2022

ISBN: 978-93-5447-311-1
eISBN: 978-93-5447-310-4

10 9 8 7 6 5 4 3 2 1

Typeset in Adobe Devanagari by SŪRYA, New Delhi
Printed at Chaman Enterprises, New Delhi

Nandita Haksar has been a practising human rights lawyer, campaigner and teacher. She has consistently taken up the rights of refugees, both in Indian courts and internationally. She has developed courses on refugee law for law colleges as well as set precedence in refugee law. She is now a full-time writer and has authored more than 15 books dealing with various aspects of nationalism and human rights, among them, *The Judgement That Never Came: Army Rule in Northeast India* (co-authored with Sebastian Hongray); *The Many Faces of Kashmiri Nationalism: From the Cold War to the Present Day*; *The Exodus Is Not Over: Migrations from the Ruptured Homelands of Northeast India*; *Kuknalim—Naga Armed Resistance: Testimonies of Leaders, Pastors, Healers and Soldiers* (co-authored with Sebastian Hongray) and *The Flavours of Nationalism: A Memoir, with Recipes for Love, Hate and Friendship.*

CONTENTS

INTRODUCTION

Refugees Are People, Not Statistics

The United Nations Refugee Agency, UNHCR, estimated that 4.5 million Iraqis had been displaced in a four-year period beginning just before the 2003 US invasion of Iraq—2.2 million crossed international borders and 2.3 million were internally displaced. In February 2007, UN High Commissioner for Refugees, António Guterres, declared the exodus of Iraqis the largest population shift in the Middle East since the displacement of Palestinians following the establishment of the state of Israel.

As of early 2022, over 9.2 million Iraqis are internally displaced or refugees abroad. Each of them has suffered pain, loss and multiple tragedies. Every story needs to be told; each tragedy needs to be recorded and remembered.

Yet, what has happened to the Iraqi refugees? They have been forgotten. They are not on anybody's priority list.

This is the story of two Iraqi brothers who were forced to leave their home and country and take refuge in India. Their story would probably not have come to be known had they not been driven by circumstances to camp outside the gate of the UNHCR office in Delhi and demand resettlement; it was a protest against the world that had forgotten them.

In documenting the story of these two young men, I discovered many aspects of India's history and its connections with Iraq. So this is also a story of a lost friendship between our two countries, our peoples.

I met the two brothers outside the gate of the UNHCR office in November 2021. I had gone there after reading about Afghan refugees who had been protesting for days, demanding to be listened to. It was really a gesture of solidarity. The day I went, I witnessed an angry demonstration by refugees demanding to speak to someone in the UNHCR office. I heard an Afghan woman shout: "If you can talk to the Taliban, why can't you talk to us?"

But the majority of the refugees gathered there on that day were not from Afghanistan but from Africa. Then I noticed that close to the cold yellow metal barriers designed to keep the refugees at bay were a few small tents. I learnt that some refugees had been camping on the road outside the UNHCR office for the past few months; among them were the two Iraqis whose story is told in this book.

I invited some of the refugees to my home, which is a short distance from the UNHCR office. The Iraqi brothers came over, and they said I reminded them of their grandmother. And so it was that I acquired two grandsons. In a way, this book is an appeal by a grandmother for the future of her grandsons.

BABIL AND AKKAD

While they wanted their story to be heard, the two brothers did not want to reveal their identities in the book, in case their family in Iraq suffered any repercussions.

We had an interesting conversation on the names by which they would be known in these pages. At first they thought of taking names from *One Thousand and One Nights*, such as Aladdin and Sindbad. Finally, they settled for Babil (Babylon) and Akkad (Akkadian empire), after the ancient empires that once flourished in the land between the Euphrates and the Tigris, the region which was famous as Mesopotamia.

Calling themselves Babil and Akkad was a way of asserting their claim over their rich heritage—from ancient, pre-Islamic times to modern Iraq; a heritage which was subjected to intentional acts of violence and destruction by Daesh* in Iraq and Syria. The destruction of ancient archaeological sites was justified by Daesh on

---

*ISIL has its origins in the Iraq War of 2003–11. Al-Qaeda in Iraq (AQI), its direct precursor, was one of the central actors in a larger Sunni insurgency against the Iraqi government and foreign occupying

religious grounds but the insurgent group has in fact used the looting as a moneymaking venture—through the illegal trade in antiquities—to finance its military operations.

The destruction of ancient Mesopotamia, land of the two rivers, is felt the world over, for, in the words of the Iraqi archaeologist Behnam Abu Al-Soof (1931-2012), "anyone who can read and write or who tills the soil, anyone who cherishes religion, practices law, or studies the stars, owes a silent thanks to those who pioneered along the Euphrates."

A report by RASHID (Research, Assessment and Safeguarding of the Heritage of Iraq in Danger) states: "The lives of individuals may compose the body of a people, but their culture represents its soul."

INDIA AND IRAQ

The day I called Babil and Akkad to my home, I had also called some of the other refugees and they too had come. We all had a meal together. But it was only the Iraqi brothers who trusted me from the beginning; our bond was immediate and special. I believe it is rooted in a history that is now largely forgotten.

---

forces. The group combined with several smaller militant groups and rebranded itself as the Islamic State of Iraq (ISI), Islamic State in Iraq and the Levant (ISIL), Arabic Arabic acronym Dāʿish or Daesh and, since June 2014, the Islamic State (IS). Daesh turned an insurgency against US troops in Iraq into a Shia–Sunni civil war.

Two years before I was born, India and Iraq signed the Treaty of Perpetual Peace and Friendship, 1952. Later, India was among the first to recognize the Ba'ath Party-led government after Iraq became a republic in 1958, following a coup that overthrew the monarchy. I grew up reading *al 'arab*, the journal of the League of Arab States Mission brought out from Link House in Delhi, and for me, the Iraqi Republic was an example of a country which prided itself on its cultural and social diversity. More than that, it represented secular Arab nationalism. At one time Iraq also had the largest communist party in the Arab world, and in 1972 it signed a 15-year Treaty of Friendship and Cooperation with the Soviet Union (around the same time that India, too, signed a similar treaty). In response, the US began to covertly finance Kurdish rebels in Iraq.

To me and many others outside Iraq, the country's achievements in the late 1960s and through the '70s appeared to be linked to the regime of Saddam Hussein (1937-2006). It was much later that I learnt a lot about the dark side of that regime and the man. Saddam became President of Iraq in 1979, but had in fact been the country's de facto leader for several years. He and the Ba'ath Party initiated reforms that were revolutionary for the Middle East. In the early 1970s, Saddam nationalized the Iraq Petroleum Company and independent banks. He fostered the modernization of the economy and gave the country social services that were unprecedented in the Arab world. Largely under Saddam's auspices, the government established universal free schooling up to the highest education level and hundreds of thousands learned to read in the years that followed. Iraq also created one of the most modernized public health systems in the Middle East, earning Saddam an award from the United Nations Educational, Scientific and Cultural Organization (UNESCO). Women in the republic had freedom and liberty, unlike women in other parts of the region.

Babil and Akkad do not understand my ambiguous attitude towards Saddam Hussein, the man they look upon as the cause of much of their suffering and pain. But I remember how close the ties were between India and Iraq during his time. In 1974, when he was Vice President, he visited India and Indira Gandhi went to receive him at the airport. When Sanjay Gandhi died in an air crash, Saddam quoted a verse from the Quran to comfort the grieving mother, whom he called his sister.

India and Indians played a significant role in Iraq's modernization. In the 1970s, there were around 80,000 Indians in Iraq, many of them doctors, lecturers and engineers. One teacher who taught mathematics in Mosul was the father of Ajaz Ashraf, now a senior journalist. Ashraf, who went on many visits to Iraq then, recalls: "Indians were respected precisely because they played a significant role in Iraq's project to emerge as a modern nation-state. They held a slew of technical teaching positions in Iraq's universities, manned its healthcare systems, built its roads and rail links, rejuvenated its agriculture, and trained its air force pilots. These roles the Indians have [also] played elsewhere, but in Iraq rarely were they looked down upon, as they are in some [other] West Asian countries.... Indians driving out of cities were often waved past check-posts without a security search, an astonishing concession from the paranoid police system that Iraq decidedly was.

"Perhaps their respect for Indians was because of the common sensibilities ancient civilizations are said to spawn. It was this sharing of sensibilities which perhaps explains the popularity of Hindi films in Iraq. They were a rage, a new release drawing packed halls. My most enduring image of their love for Hindi cinema is the audience response to a scene in *Sholay*. It was that dramatic shot in which Gabbar Singh, after mowing down Thakur's family, points the gun at his grandson trembling in fear. The audience burst out shouting, 'No, no,' and took to hurling Coke-bottle caps at the screen. You would have thought the Iraqis were incapable of fighting one bloody war after another."*

---

*https://www.firstpost.com/world/iraq-and-india-a-forgotten-love-story-1581885.html

Saddam Hussein became the fifth president of Iraq in 1979, the year that saw the Islamic Revolution in Iran. The next year Iraq invaded Iran and the Iran-Iraq war lasted eight long years. Iraq's primary rationale for the invasion was to cripple Iran and prevent Ruhollah Khomeini from exporting the Islamic Revolution to Shia-majority Iraq and exploit religious tensions. Iraq also aspired to replace Iran as the dominant state in the Persian Gulf.

At the time, I was a research student in Jawaharlal Nehru University (JNU), Delhi, and recall the terror in the eyes of the Iranian students with left and communist leanings who were being deported to the post-revolution Iran. A number of fellow students rose in their support, literally holding on to them and preventing some deportations. Even among those who did not support the Iraqi invasion, there were mixed feelings.

When I told Babil and Akkad all this, they heard me in silence and then Babil commented wryly: "You liked Saddam because you have not lived in Iraq."

Babil and Akkad arrived in India in 2014. It was the year that a Hindu nationalist party was voted into power in India. It was also the year that Daesh launched an offensive on Mosul and Tikrit. And on June 29, 2014, the Daesh leader Abu Bakr al-Baghdadi announced the formation of a caliphate stretching from Aleppo in Syria to Diyala in Iraq, and renamed the group the

Islamic State (IS).*

It was the same year that Indian television news channels reported the kidnapping of 40 Indians by Daesh in Mosul; 39 would be killed.

Both India and Iraq had changed, and Third World solidarity was a distant memory.

In order to understand the political and historical forces that led to Babil and Akkad becoming refugees, we would have to know not only the history of Iraq but also the role of many other countries, including the US, in the tragedy that is still unfolding in Iraq. I had come to understand some of this about 25 years ago.

We also need to understand aspects of the Indian law and the processes of the UNHCR and other refugee agencies.

IRAQI REFUGEES IN INDIA, 1998

Before I met Babil and Akkad I had occasion to take up the case of two other Iraqi brothers in 1998. I was living in Goa and the UNHCR contacted me sometime in August that year to say that two Iraqi men were being held at the Vasco Police Station and would I interview them to see if they came under the definition of refugees and merited UNHCR protection.

---

*At its peak in January 2015, ISIL covered an area across Syria and Iraq roughly equivalent to the size of the UK and attracted 40,000 foreign fighters to its cause. https://www.aljazeera.com/news/2019/10/27/who-was-isils-self-proclaimed-leader-abu-bakr-al-baghdadi

That is how I met Hazim Adeem Hussain, who was about 28 then, and his brother Anwar, 21.

Hazeem and Anwar's father and elder brother had opposed Saddam's regime and were arrested, detained and executed sometime after the first Gulf War in 1991. Their home was blown up and the family scattered. Hazim and Anwar escaped to Iran around 1991-92. They survived in hiding there and tried to get to Europe.

They went to the Iranian port of Bander Abbas, looking for a ship on which they could escape as stowaways. They were excited when they found a ship going to Vasco, thinking it was a destination in Europe. They hid aboard the ship, *MV Ratnadeep*, in April 1997 and survived on vitamin tablets. By the time they arrived in Goa on May 9, 1997, Anwar had tuberculosis. Things got worse. They were arrested for entering India illegally as stowaways.

Hazim described how, in the Goan jail, he had a wonderful experience when someone told him that it was Eid and offered him a small carpet to pray. The other inmates, mostly Hindus, joined him as he led the prayers. This seemed to confirm what they had heard about India when they were growing up, that it was a nation of religious tolerance.

In April 1998 they completed their jail term but could not be set free since they did not have proper travel documents. The jail authorities did not understand their political situation and as a matter of routine informed the Iraqi embassy; an embassy official then visited them in jail which made them fear for their lives in case they were deported. Their only hope was to get the protection of the UNHCR.

It took me some time to get this story from Hazim, whose knowledge of English was limited. Anwar had refused to learn any English at all because he saw it as the language of the hated Americans.

The police officer in charge was sympathetic and allowed Hazim to leave the police station and meet me, but Anwar was kept as a hostage. Their case was pending in court, but just after our meeting, a magistrate passed an order to deport the brothers.

I filed a writ petition before the Goa Bench of the Bombay High Court. There was considerable excitement in the court because it was probably the first such refugee case. I overheard a lawyer remark that there was no refugee law in India so how could I expect the protection of the courts. However, I was quite clear that even foreigners have rights under Article 21 (life and liberty) and Article 14 (arbitrariness of state action) of the Indian Constitution.

But the judges were unwilling to listen to Constitutional arguments, or even to examine the orders of the Gauhati High Court in cases I had filed some years ago on behalf of refugees from Burma. The Gauhati High Court had allowed the Burmese to seek UNHCR protection.

The judges in Goa were conservative and so were the lawyers in the court. I could feel the full impact of the prejudice and hostility towards "outsiders"; not only my clients but I too evoked hostility. One judge voiced his real fear: the two brothers were Muslims from Iraq and could be terrorists. My petition was dismissed and I could see the smirks on the faces of several lawyers.

Hazim was distraught. I was angry. I phoned the UNHCR and spoke to the Legal Officer for an hour. This, perhaps, was the case I argued most forcefully and passionately. In the end, the Legal Officer agreed to give Hazim and Anwar certificates of "under consideration", and that is how they were finally released from police custody. They then left for Delhi, so that they could seek the protection of the UNHCR.

The night before they left, we tried to give some money to Hazim but he refused to take it. I think we used the word "help" which Hazim interpreted to mean "charity" and he could not, he would never, accept charity. We had no way of explaining that "solidarity" was what we meant. But I knew Hazim had spent all of the little money he had in making sherbets for us and also biryani for our friends. So I sat down with him and Anwar and explained that they were now part of our family and I had every right to give money to younger members of my family. Hazim smiled and finally accepted the money.

It was this same deep-rooted self-respect that

stopped Babil and Akkad, almost a quarter century later, from asking for financial assistance even from the UNHCR. They found ways to support themselves. But after the COVID pandemic reached India and there were a series of lockdowns, this became impossible. Their already precarious lives were devastated and it was then that they decided to protest outside the UNHCR office and demand that they be resettled in a third country because Indian law prohibited them from working legally or even opening a bank account.

In order to get a residential permit, refugees in India recognized by the UNHCR have to go to the Foreigners Regional Registration Office (FRRO), which has the power to issue a residential permit or even a long-term visa. In 1998, when Hazim and Anwar reached Delhi and went to register themselves with the FRRO, they were instead arrested. The police sent them to the Lampur detention camp on the Delhi-Haryana border. This was despite the fact that they were refugees recognized by the UNHCR.

Hazim and Anwar had gone to the FRRO in the company of a Burmese refugee Soe Myint (on my insistence), and he phoned to tell me what had happened. I requested a lawyer friend in Delhi to get the two brothers out of detention and ensure they were not deported. After their release from jail Hazim wrote to me about their experience and his words speak of the ordeal despite the problem of syntax:

> Regarding the problem we had with the FRRO I will explain it—when I and Sumit [he means Soe Myint] went their (sic) and the officer we met was of a bad manners, he quarreled with us and told us to go to the Home Ministry and then we went to Home Ministry again with Harsh's friend [this was a friend in JNU who had volunteered to teach the Iraqis English] they gave us a sealed envelope to the FRRO then we were arrested and sent to Jail on 24/09/98/ on the same day they tortured us because they had orders from the FRRO then they fought with Anwar. I told them my brother is sick One police man took a stick and beat me with it, I said it does not matter, for I hit them they will beat us even more after a short time four police man came and took us into other room and beat us and I believe me I did not beat anybody till he hit me on the operation of my hands. It was so painful and became blue so I bite him back They after five days registered a case against us and jailed us but we passed the ordeal with Almighty's help and your help that all.

I learnt from my lawyer friends in Delhi that Hafiz and Anwar's was not an isolated case. Muslim refugees were being rounded up and thrown into the Lampur detention centre. It goes without saying that the conditions there were abysmal. Even today this practice continues; even refugees recognized by the UNHCR are sent to Lumpur and then deported. This is a violation of the principle of non-refoulement. The Courts define non-refoulement as "a principle of international law that provides a refugee or asylum seeker with the right to freedom from expulsion from a territory in which he or she seeks refuge or from forcible return to a country or a territory where he or she faces a threat to life". Although India does not have a refugee law, the principle of non-refoulement has been recognized by the courts as a part of the right to life.

With the help of lawyers and friends in JNU, I got Hazim and Anwar out but the UNHCR should have provided this service to the refugees under their protection. And the FRRO should have informed the UNHCR that they had detained a refugee who was under the protection of the UNHCR.

In December 2021, the Convenor of Indian Friends of Refugees, N.D. Pancholi, tried to get information under the Right to Information (RTI) Act on how many UNHCR recognized refugees have been deported from India. The Government replied that India was not a signatory to the UN Refugee Convention. This is their reply of January 2022:

No. 25022/1/RTI/2022-F.IV
Government of India
Ministry of Home Affairs
Foreigner Division
*****

1st Floor, Major Dhyan Chand National Stadium
New Delhi, dated 5th January, 2022

To

Shri N.D. Pancholi,
F-1/A-75, Shalimar garden Main,
Sahibabad, Ghaziabad,
Pin: 201008, Uttar Pradesh.

Subject: Information sought by Shri N.D. Pancholi under The RTI Act, 2005.

Sir,

Please refer to your online RTI application bearing Registration No. MHOME/R/P/21/01553 dated 22-12-2021 seeking information under the RTI Act, 2005.

2. The information is furnished as under:

Query No.	**Information sought**	**Information**
1.	How many refugees recognized by the United Nations High Commissioner For Refugees (UNHCR) have been deported to their country of origin in the past five years? From which countries were these refugees from?	India is not a signatory to the 1951 UN Convention relating to the Status of Refugees and the 1967 Protocol thereon. All foreign nationals (including refuge seekers) are governed by the provisions contained in The Foreigners Act, 1946, The Registration of Foreigners Act, 1939, The Passport (Entry into India) Act, 1920 and The Citizenship Act, 1955 and rules and orders made thereunder. Necessary action for deportation of foreign nationals is taken by the State Government/UT Administrations concerned as well as by Bureau of Immigration under their delegated powers. You may therefore approach the State Governments/UT Administrations for getting the desired information. The RTI application is also being transferred to the Bureau of Immigration under Section 6(3) of the RTI Act, 2005, for providing the available information (if any).
2.	Was UNHCR informed before the deportation of such refugees?	
3.	Does Indian not respect the right to non refoulement of UNHCR recognized refugees?	

3. As per Section 19 of RTI Act, 2005, the First Appellate Authority is Shri Sumant Singh, Joint Secretary (Foreigners), Ministry of Home Affairs, Major Dhyan Chand National Stadium, New Delhi- 110001, before whom First Appeal may be preferred within the time limit specified in the RTI Act, 2005.

Then N.D. Pancholi went in appeal, and this time the Intelligence Bureau replied, claiming exemption from answering the question. Here is the letter from the Intelligence Bureau:

Regd. AD

No. 8/Imm/2022 (01)/VOL-03 – 372
INTELLIGENCE BUREAU
(Ministry of Home Affairs)
Government of India
****

New Delhi, dated 10|2|.2022

To

Sh. N. D. Pancholi
F-1/A-75, Shalimar Garden Main
Sahibabad, Ghaziabad
Uttar Pradesh- 201008

Sub: **Your RTI application seeking information on refugees recognized by UNHCR & their deportation under RTI Act 2005.**

Please refer to your RTI application dated 17/12/2021 transferred by the Ministry of Home Affairs vide their letter dated 05/01/2022 (received in this office on 12/01/2022) on the above cited subject.

2 It is mentioned that sought information partially pertains to Bureau of Immigration (BoI)/Intelligence Bureau (IB). However, as per Chapter VI, Section 24 (1) and Second Schedule of the RTI Act 2005, BoI/IB is exempted from providing any information / details on the subject.

3. In case you are not satisfied with the above reply, you may file an appeal with the Appellate Authority, Sh. Sandeep Sharma, Deputy Director, IB, Level-7, East Block-8, R. K. Puram, New Delhi-110066 within 30 days of receipt of this letter by you.

(U.K. Sinha)
Assistant Director
& CPIO

Copy to Sh. Ram Dayal Meena, Director (F) & CPIO, MHA, Foreigners Division, 1st Floor, Major Dhyan Chand National Stadium, New Delhi w.r.t. letter No. 25022/1/RTI/2021-F.IV dated 05/01/2022.

I had to go to Delhi soon after Hazim and Anwar were released from jail when my father passed away in November 1998. The brothers came for my father's memorial meeting. Hazim brought a huge *thali* of an exotic Iraqi sweetmeat; he said that this was the tradition in Iraq. Anwar helped me with the flower arrangements.

Twenty-three years later, when Babil and Akkad brought me a box of Iraqi sweets for Diwali, I could see that the basic values were the same. But something had changed from the time Hazim and Anwar came to India.

At that time too Iraqi refugees were not given much financial assistance by the UNHCR and they faced great hardship because they could not legally work. But Hazim and Anwar found support among the other Iraqi refugees—some 70 Iraqi refugees, including women and children, had decided to go on an indefinite hunger strike outside the UNHCR office in support of their demand for resettlement in some other country.

The UNHCR had already become very bureaucratic. When I first contacted the agency back in 1990 it had felt like a safe harbour for refugees, but by 1998 even a lawyer like me who had been doing refugee cases pro bono for so many years could not get easy access to the Legal Officer, let alone the Chief of Mission. In the evenings, my husband and I would go to the Iraqi refugees' campaign outside the UNHCR office with some hot tea in the biting cold of a Delhi winter and sit with them for an hour or two.

It was after a bitter struggle that the UNHCR finally agreed to resettle Hazim, Anwar and all the other Iraqi refugees in Europe. I was not in Delhi when Hazim and Anwar flew to Sweden. But Hazim phoned to say he would return one day. Sometime after they had reached Sweden, I got a call from Hazim. He said: "I don't like Sweden, they don't like people with black hair."

Then we lost touch. But I had preserved their file and now, 23 years later, I showed it to Babil and Akkad.

When I asked Babil and Akkad why the Iraqi refugees in India could not come together and protest jointly again, they said they did not trust one another. The sectarian divide had had such a deep impact on the entire population that it could not be surmounted even when they were hundreds of miles away from their country and should have been united in their common hardship and suffering.

REFUGEES FROM A HYBRID WAR

Even though their father and brother had been executed by Saddam Hussein, Hazim and Anwar had been clear that it was the Iraqis who must get rid of the dictator, no matter how hard that appeared to be. They were opposed to US invasion of their country. In contrast, Babil and Akkad belonged to a generation which had seen so many wars and conflicts that they thought that if the US invaded and got rid of Saddam Hussein, all would be well and Iraq would have peace and security.

Yet, nearly two decades after the US invasion in 2003, when Saddam was captured and executed, Iraq is no closer to becoming a peaceful country that refugees like Babil and Akkad can return to.

Babil and Akkad had not heard of the whistleblower Chelsea Manning, a US Army soldier, or Julian Assange of Wikileaks, who exposed the lies and cynical politics behind the invasion of Iraq. They did not know that multiple CIA reports had dismissed the claim that Iraq and Al-Qaeda were cooperating; or that the United States Senate Report on Pre-war Intelligence on Iraq had concluded that many of the Bush Administration's statements about Iraqi Weapons of Mass Destruction were either false or misleading. Even if they had, they would still have seen things differently. Many people, like me, see the tragedy of Iraq as a product of US policy, but for Babil and Akkad it is not at all so clear. Besides, they were just children when their country became the site of a hybrid war.

While it is true that Saddam Hussein's Ba'athist regime in Iraq was violent and oppressive, what replaced it proved to be even worse. Far from affecting only Iraqis, the US invasion of Iraq has had global repercussions. A report of the International Crisis Group points out the cynical and destructive ways in which the US administration manipulated Iraqi social, sectarian, ethnic and tribal divisions for its own gains.

These manipulations led to a plethora of extremist

groups entering Iraq, from the Mahdi Army and militias loyal to the Islamic Republic of Iran's Revolutionary Guard Corps (IRGC) and Daesh. The invasion of Iraq led to a regional spillover that has also engulfed Europe with a refugee crisis, and revived far-right and isolationist tendencies in the West. And now Iraqi refugees like Babil and Akkad are finding it difficult to get resettlement in the Europe or North America.

This is precisely a characteristic of hybrid wars.

Hybrid warfare is a theory of political military strategy which blends conventional warfare, irregular warfare and cyber warfare with other influencing methods such as fake news, diplomacy, lawfare, business and foreign electoral intervention. A telling instance is a case in a US court wherein the plaintiffs contend that the militant group Jaysh al-Mahdi controlled Iraq's health ministry and that 21 defendant medical companies, including AstraZeneca and Pfizer, made corrupt payments to obtain medical supply contracts.

By combining kinetic operations with subversive efforts, the aggressor intends to avoid attribution or retribution. There is no invader; no nation and its allies are to blame for mass murder, for destroying entire countries and societies. No one needs to take responsibility for the refugees of a hybrid war.

There are other repercussions. The US offered some protection—from the violent and tragic chaos it had created—to those Iraqis who were directly employed by its mission and other organizations. Babil and Akkad had an aunt who had been a translator for the Americans. She and her family have been given asylum in the US. Were Babil and Akkad to return to their country now, this fact alone could get them killed.

UNHCR INDIFFERENCE

The UNHCR is supposed to find permanent solutions to the refugee problem. But, as far as Babil and Akkad are concerned, all they have received are identity cards recognizing them as refugees under the mandate of the UNHCR. They have been renewing their cards every two years.

The UNHCR has arranged for some basic English language classes, help in getting low-paid informal, intermittent jobs and, after the second phase of the pandemic, some rations. But no financial assistance, even for medical expenses, has ever been given.

In fact, now the UNHCR does not even meet the refugees inside the office. Its staff and representatives stand outside and talk to the refugees or sit in a park and make assurances which have no legal backing.

Now Babil and Akkad are demanding that the UNHCR arrange for their resettlement in another country where they will be allowed to work legally and rebuild their lives. The uncertainty of their future and the stress of trying to survive has taken a toll on them; added to which is the fact that they have no medical help in coping with the trauma of losing their father and being sent away to a foreign country.

Their case for resettlement falls squarely in the category of "lack of foreseeable alternative durable solution". It also falls in the category of cases that need treatment for psychological trauma but they do not have access to the treatment; and till the state of uncertainty exists, the possibility of cure is limited.

INDIA AND REFUGEES

India was once a country which welcomed refugees from all parts of the world. The Constitution of India guarantees two rights to foreigners, even those who come into India illegally: the right to life (Article 21) and the right to equality before the law (Article 14). India is also a signatory to various international human rights treaties under which human rights of refugees are protected.

The courts in India have protected refugees from being deported and allowed them to seek the protection of the UNHCR. But in recent years refugees are finding that their UNHCR identity cards are not being respected and do not protect them from arbitrary detentions and even police atrocities. Increasingly, the refugee is looked upon just as an illegal person with no rights. In many countries the 'No One is Illegal' movement has helped protect refugees, but in India there is very little support for refugees from civil society.

There is no tradition of people inviting refugees to their homes, and for most Indians the refugees remain invisible and an unimportant factor in our national life. More recently, there has been clear and often vicious, officially sanctioned discrimination against Muslim refugees.

These are the circumstances which forced the two Iraqi brothers to protest outside the UNHCR office in August 2021.

DREAMING OF A HOME

When I met Akkad outside the UNHCR office, he said that all he wanted was to have a family of his own and a home to come back to. It is a simple dream. International human rights treaties protect the right to family, the right to work, the right to mental health and decent standards of living. Babil and Akkad have been denied all these rights by the UNHCR and the Indian State.

When I invited all the refugees camping outside the UNHCR office in Delhi to my home, all the others were suspicious of my motives; they wondered why I, a non-Muslim, would care. In contrast, Babil said I reminded him of his grandmother. He said he felt at home in my flat. My husband and I opened up our home to Babil and Akkad and they have become part of our family.

But I do not have the ability to protect them; in

the eyes of the law, Babil and Akkad are just illegal foreigners liable to be deported.

I am amazed at how the brothers have preserved their ability to laugh. They still watch cartoons, enjoy a barbeque and retain the capacity to love and care. And together we are discovering the many connections between India and Iraq.

First of all, we have stories that connect us. We have all grown up listening to the tales from *One Thousand and One Nights*. I had heard them from my mother in Hindi; but Babil insisted we watch an old animation of Sindibad in Arabic. The film was made in 1947. We both exclaimed with delight when we saw that the Emir was being entertained by an Indian magician and a snake charmer.

Then Babil recalled his parents reading some Indian animal stories in Arabic, *Kalila and Dimna*. He had found the book in my library. I told him the stories were from the *Panchtantra* and originally written in Sanskrit. The earliest known translation from Sanskrit into a non-Indian language is in Middle Persian (Pahlavi, 550 CE) by Burzoe. This became the basis for a Syriac translation as *Kalilag and Damnag* and a translation into Arabic in 750 CE by Persian scholar Abdullah Ibn al-Muqaffa as *Kalīlah wa Dimnah*. *Kalila and Dimna* is considered a masterpiece of Arabic and world literature, being one of the most popular and seminal books ever written. It forms part of Arab pop culture today and remains widely read in the Arab world.

The protest outside the UNHCR inspired some of us lawyers to come together and form the Indian Friends of Refugees. So, already, Babil and Akkad's story has the power to bring people together.

I hope that their story, told in the pages that follow, will lead them to a safe harbour where they can have a home and families of their own. And I hope that they will return to Iraq one day. I hope they will tell their children and grandchildren of their adventures in distant lands.

NANDITA HAKSAR

January 15, 2022

The Story of the Iraqi Brothers

(As told to Nandita Haksar)

PRELUDE

The Importance of Remembering

We want to tell our story but we do not remember many dates, even some years. Before we came to India and became refugees, we started to forget our home, our friends and even our family. Over these years we both became aware that we are suffering memory loss. Perhaps it is just too painful to recall the trauma and pain we have been through.

When you are 26 years old and travelling in a plane for the first time, it should be an exciting experience, an adventure. Like the adventures of Sindbad that I had seen on television. But the flight from Baghdad to Hyderabad seven years ago was memorable for all the wrong reasons. My younger brother and I were leaving our mother, our home and our country to become refugees.

My father had been kidnapped just a few weeks before. And now the same people who had taken him were looking for us. But who were they? We never came to know. Iraq was full of militias, it was impossible to tell. We were forced into hiding and, soon after, we were given our passports with visas for India, a country about which we knew next to nothing.

We could not say goodbye to our mother; we could not hug her one last time. We had no idea how long we would be gone. It was all a terrible nightmare, but we still felt we would wake up and find ourselves back home with our parents soon.

We did not know the nightmare had only just begun and that it would go on for years…and memories of our homeland would slowly begin to fade. Only raw, searing emotion would remain. The pain of loss, the alienation stemming from being in a strange country where we were unwanted, we had no rights and where we could not belong no matter how hard we tried. We were considered "illegal" foreigners without any legal protection.

Our only glimmer of hope was the UNHCR and we had so much respect for it and expectations. After all, its work was protecting people like us—people the international community calls "refugees".

This book is our story, of two brothers, and the circumstances that forced us to become refugees. We cannot reveal our names because of the danger of repercussions for our family in Iraq.

In a way, our names do not matter. Because our story is also the story of thousands of fellow Iraqis who have been forced to leave our country. And it is the story of how the world has chosen to forget us.

Therefore, it is important for us to remember. As the Sufi scholar SheikhIsmail Hakki said:

> Everything is dependent upon remembering. One does not begin by learning, one starts by remembering. The distance of eternal existence and the difficulties of life cause one to forget.
>
> It is for this reason God has commanded us: "Remember!"

BABIL AND AKKAD

January 2022

1

THE CHILDREN OF IRAQ HAVE NAMES

The children of Iraq have names.
They are not the nameless ones.
The children of Iraq have names.
Their names are not collateral damage.

—David Krieger (2002)

Babil was born in January 1988, seven months before the Iraq-Iran war ended with a stalemate—both sides claiming victory. Tensions between Iraq and Iran were fuelled by Iran's Islamic revolution and its appearance of being a pan-Islamic force, in contrast to Iraq's Arab nationalism led by the Arab Socialist Ba'ath Party.

Akkad was born in April 1991, four months after the Gulf War started: a war waged by coalition forces from 35 nations led by the United States in response to Iraq's invasion and annexation of Kuwait arising from oil pricing and production disputes.

The sanctions against Iraq were a near-total financial and trade embargo imposed by the United Nations Security Council. They came into effect on August 6, 1990, four days after Iraq's *invasion of Kuwait, and stayed in force until 2003, when Saddam Hussein was captured by US troops.*

BABIL

It is true the children of Iraq have names, but many cannot reveal them because the revelation could lead to their deaths or the kidnapping of their loved ones. And so it is with us, two Iraqi brothers who dare not write under our own names even though we are so far from the home we were forced to leave.

This is the first time I am telling my story and perhaps it will help me put things in some perspective.

I was born in January 1988, seven months before the Iraq-Iran war ended in a stalemate though each side claimed victory. I do not have personal memories of that war.

But there is one story that I was told so often that I think of it as part of my own memory. It is a story of how my grandfather, my mother's father who lived in Baghdad, managed to procure a banana for me, his grandson. It was an event so memorable that the story has been preserved in our family like a precious heirloom. The war had left our family, like so many families across the country, utterly devastated. There was never enough food to eat and to gift a child a banana became a big event and a memorable one.

I have been told the story of the banana so many times that when I saw the Minions singing the Banana Song in *Despicable Me 2*, I remembered how my grandfather had managed to get a banana for me in the midst of the war.

Although I do not remember the gift of the banana, I do remember asking my mother to buy me an ice-cream and her reply that she could not afford it.

At that time I did not ask why we could not afford to buy ice-creams or bananas even though Baba, my father, was a qualified engineer and had a good job. We lived in a well-appointed housing complex with modern amenities. It was not only the wars that had affected our living standards, the sanctions imposed on Iraq had pushed us deeper into such a dire condition.

Despite living through not one but several wars, my memories of my childhood are sunny and bright. When I look back, I think it is amazing that I have so many happy memories of my family, my friends, my school and our home.

My earliest memories are from the time we lived in Al-Iskandriya, which in ancient times stood halfway between Babylon (where Alexander died) and Seleucia on the Tigris. Seleucia, the capital of the Seleucid Empire, was very near to modern Baghdad. My father worked at the Hateen Munitions Complex.

When I was around two years old, on August 2, 1990, the Iraqi Army invaded and occupied Kuwait. And my brother Akkad was born soon after in April 1991.

It was much later that I learnt the war was called the Video Game War; we called it the *aleudwan althalathiniu* or the aggression by thirty nations.

I was barely three years old but I do remember the sound of a bomb exploding one morning while we were having breakfast. My mother said the sound of planes used to frighten me and I could not sleep at night.

She described how Baba made me feel safe even amidst the bombing. He would hold me as I lay with my head resting on his shoulder. With his hand he would make a gesture of a plane flying and gently mimic the sound of it going over my head. Mama said my eyes were wide with terror. Then Baba would make another booming sound and say, "See, the planes have all gone and we have won the war." And I would close my eyes, feeling safe in my father's arms, and fall asleep.

My parents did all they could to protect me from the harsh realities of the war and the shortage of food. But I know it was a really hard time for them. There was never enough food and my parents often went without eating so that they could give us a meal. Mama had to go to a nearby stream to collect drinking water since the water pipeline had been destroyed. But the stream water was not really fit for drinking.

One day, Akkad and I were going somewhere with

friends; we were both wearing new clothes and shoes. Then Akkad stepped into mud and his sandals got soiled. I took him to the edge of the stream and was scooping out water with my hands to clean his sandals when a friend playfully shoved me into the stream. I did not know swimming but managed to catch hold of the roots of a tree and haul myself out of the water. My clothes and shoes were all wet and dirty because the stream water was unclean.

During the war the furnace in my father's factory was hit by a rocket and it went up in flames. My father and his team of engineers got it working again. I do not know the details but he was given an award by the President. I remember watching Baba on television and feeling so happy and proud. We had the President's certificate in our house but later we tore it up.

Possessing a certificate signed by Saddam Hussein could have got us into trouble with the Americans who came regularly to search our homes; and it would also have got us into trouble with the militias who too hated him. Our family did not support the Ba'ath Party but it was a certificate of appreciation given by the President of our country!

Soon after, we moved to another small town in western Iraq which was a short distance from Fallujah. Fallujah too dates back to Babylonian times and hosted important Jewish academies for many centuries. The city is in Al Anbar province, 69 km west of Baghdad, on the Euphrates river. It was a Sunni-dominated province and we were Shias. But in those days these things did not matter.

My father worked as an engineer for the defence establishment. We lived in a beautiful house within a modern residential complex built to international standards. The complex had about 500 housing units, a mix of independent houses and apartments. It was considered an integrated neighbourhood in all respects, with modern markets, schools, kindergartens, a general hospital and recreational facilities such as an outdoor swimming pool, a sports club.

Some people called the housing complex "mini Iraq" because it represented diverse segments of the Iraqi population with different nationalities, sects, religions and origins.

The wars and the economic sanctions had devastated our country and, despite living in this modern housing complex with all these amenities, we had to face great economic hardship. By the end of the Iran-Iraq war, my father could afford to buy only a bag of tomatoes with his salary. My parents had to find ways to earn more money. They started making kibbeh, or kubba as we call it in Iraq.

Kibbeh is a family of dishes based on spiced and ground meat, onions and grain, popular in Middle Eastern cuisine. There are many ways of making kubba, the type my parents made was Kubba el Mosul. Kubba is usually made by pounding bulgur (cracked wheat) together with meat into a fine paste and forming it into balls with toasted pine nuts and spices. It can also be layered and cooked on a tray, deep-fried, grilled, or served raw.

My parents made the kubba at home and then they gave it to a shop in the shopping complex to sell.

I remember seeing Mama and Baba in the kitchen, making the kubba. It was hard work. My father was an expert in making the meatballs and I recall him sweating so much that I took him a towel to wipe his face. For me these are happy memories because I was with my parents, helping them.

At first we lived in a house allotted by the government. It had a big garden with fruit trees, including apricot, pomegranate, date and olive. And we had a big buckthorn tree which used to have branches which would grow to the height of our roof and we could pick the sweet berries easily. At the back of the house we had a small kitchen garden with lots of vegetables such as tomatoes, celery, carrots, radish and potatoes.

Another memory is of a small bat which came into our house. We have a legend that says a bat can come and stick onto your face and you cannot pull it off until you give it gold water. So I remember us holding cushions in front of our faces and trying to chase the bat out of the house. It grew tired of flitting around and flew out!

AKKAD

Our father also kept chickens. There was a large room behind our house where the central air conditioning unit was situated and we kept our chickens in that room.

BABIL

Yes! Baba bought chicks, ducks and geese. I used to feed the little birds and made a pond for them beside our house. I remember when the goose laid her first egg and how proudly the gander danced with his wings spread!

AKKAD

Do you remember when our home was robbed? I was very small but I recall we came back from Baghdad after celebrating Eid with our grandparents and we found our house had been robbed. Our television was gone so we could not watch cartoons.

They even took the framed family photographs. There was a photograph of my mother and me when I was a baby. I had golden hair then, it turned black later. I do not have any photographs from my childhood. They stole our memories. They even stole our Quran Sharif.

At that time it did not matter so much except for the loss of our television which meant we could not watch cartoons.

BABIL

I had forgotten about the robbery. It was a bit of a mystery why our house got robbed.

I remember that my father asked the guards how intruders could enter the house when they were on duty. The thieves used a tool to cut the glass expertly and open the door and walk away with our things. It was not the loss of material goods that upset Baba so much as the fact that someone could violate our home.

Seeing my father's expression, my little brother and I offered him all the money we had been gifted as Eidi. Father was very moved and said he would not take our money. But our mother took it from us afterwards and kept it so we learnt to save the money.

For Akkad and me the theft of the television was what upset us most. We begged Baba to buy another television because we missed watching cartoons.

Which cartoons did we watch?

I remember watching *Tom and Jerry* and the *Wonderful Adventures of Nils*. Our aunt called Akkad Nils because, like Nils, Akkad too loved animals and talked to them. The cartoons were all in Arabic. We also watched an original Arabic animation of Sindibad (that's how we pronounce the name in Arabic) the sailor.

So when our television was stolen we really missed the cartoons. Finally, Baba bought a black and white set. Every day, we waited for the cartoons and that was the time we found ourselves also watching news of the war.

The thieves had stolen our lovely oil heater too. But we found that out many days later. One day, when we were returning from Baghdad after visiting our grandparents, it was very cold and I was longing to reach home so we could sit by the heater. It was a lovely heater on which we could toast bread and even make chai. It was missing. That is when we discovered that the heater had also been stolen.

Once I had a toothache and my mother took me to a dentist. I was terrified and ran out of the hospital. My mother brought me back and the dentist told me sternly: "If you behave like this how can we rely on your generation to free Palestine?"

The next day my mother took me again and I watched a boy like me sitting calmly and having his tooth pulled out. I took courage and sat quietly in the dentist's chair. The dentist told my mother she had a very brave son!

The Iraq War ended on February 28, 1991, with a ceasefire negotiated between the UN coalition and Iraq. But our lives continued much as they had before. I have happy memories of school and playing football. I was made an assistant to the class monitor and my mother made cake so I could distribute it in my class.

This was the time when our country was still ruled by Saddam Hussein, the fifth President of Iraq and his

Ba'ath Party. The party initially consisted of a majority of Shia Muslims, but it slowly became Sunni-dominated so we grew up thinking of it as a Sunni outfit.

Mama and Baba warned us that we must never criticize our President and that even walls have ears. The name "Saddam" evoked fear in me. It was only after Saddam Hussein was captured by the US troops that I saw videos of how people were tortured by his Ba'ath Party. I also saw videos of his son Uday having parties with drinks and women. When we went to college in Baghdad I learnt how women students were terrified of being picked up by Uday.

I did not understand politics but I did see that the children whose fathers belonged to the Ba'ath Party were better off than us. They had better clothes and shoes and could eat things we could not afford.

In school we had a flag-hoisting ceremony every day. One day my name was called out. I was mortified. I was among those who had not joined the youth wing of the Ba'ath Party. I just did not want to even though my friends said I would get extra points during exams if I joined. I have always felt uncomfortable with politics.

Then my name was called out a second time. That day I was not feeling well. When I told the man who wanted to recruit me, he said they had a doctor and he would easily find out if I was lying. But I genuinely had a bad throat and was told to go home. I happily went home and told Mama what had happened.

I was afraid that they would try to force me to join the party but my name was never called out again. Mama told me not to worry because they would not bother me anymore.

I overheard her tell Baba that she had gone to the principal and told him that our President himself had said no one was to be recruited by force.

In those days we never felt any threat or fear on account of being born in a Shia family. All of us children went to the same mosque even if we Shias had a slightly different way of offering Salah or *namaaz*, as you call it here in India. We went to the same mosque and had the same kind of religious instruction.

But there was one incident which showed that there were some underlying tensions even though we were unaware of them at that time. My father had bought a flat in the housing complex so we shifted from the government house to the apartment on the ground floor. On that day, my mother was upset because the people upstairs had asked her whether she was a Shia or Sunni.

But I also have a nice memory from then. There was a garden in front of our apartment. One day I found a baby hedgehog there and brought it into the house and fed it. It was so cute. But my father said the hedgehog too must be having a family and would be missing its Mama and Baba so I should release it back.

In front of our new home, across the main street,

were salt fields where we played football and beyond that there was a stream. And beyond that lay the vast desert.

Some of my best memories are of the times when our family drove to Baghdad to my maternal grandparents' home. My father had bought a second-hand Toyota Crown Royal Saloon, 1985 model. It was red and we would pile into the car and drive off to Baghdad. It was about an hour's drive.

I was not close to my paternal grandparents. In fact, we rarely met them.

My maternal grandparents lived in a large, two-storeyed house. My mother told me that her father was hot-tempered but a good man. He had saved many people from being executed by Saddam Hussein. However, I do not remember any specific stories.

My mother's sisters would also come there and they would all cook in the kitchen. In front of my grandparents' home was a garden and at the far end was a date tree. My grandfather would shake the tree and the dates would fall on a plastic sheet. My brother and I and our cousins collected them and then my aunts would wash and clean them. Then they would put the dates into plastic bags and place a heavy weight on the bags so that the dates became one flat piece. The piece would be cut into pieces which we then shared with our neighbours.

Have you ever had dates fresh from a tree? They taste heavenly!

I was particularly close to one of my cousins. We had great fun together. He was very popular in the neighbourhood and I would play football with his friends. I remember one of the games we played—we would take mattresses and put them at the top of the stairs and then jump on them and go sliding down!

At night all of us, my uncles and aunts, my parents and grandparents, cousins and my brother and I slept on the roof. There was always a fresh breeze blowing and it was pleasant to see the clear sky above us. The stars were bright and my father would teach me their names. My uncle was in the army and he had an army telescope through which we would look at the moon. It seemed I could see the terrain. It was stunning. I recall those days and nights. I wish time had stopped then.

AKKAD

Those were indeed lovely times. I remember playing hide and seek. I would climb up the buckthorn tree and shake it so that all the berries fell. They were so sweet. We used to fly kites and I also played hopscotch which was usually played by the girls.

But when we went back home I would be reminded that everything was not normal. We knew that the US had accused Saddam Hussein of secretly storing weapons of mass destruction. We knew that UN weapons inspectors had come to Baba's office to inspect the establishment where my father worked since it was involved in defence production. They never found any weapons of mass destruction.

I was too young to understand what it all meant but I do remember the war when it started in 2003. I was around 12 years old. Before the war started, Baba bought provisions to last several months.

BABIL

We began to hear there was going to be a war. We heard the news on television. By this time we once again had a colour television set. This time we watched the war on television. To begin with it still seemed distant and unreal.

At first we did not believe there would be a war but then it became a real possibility and I heard Baba tell Mama that the war could begin any day and we should meet all our neighbours and bid everyone goodbye and ask for their forgiveness in case we had unknowingly done anything to hurt them.

Before the war started I remember being enveloped in an eerie silence during the afternoons. At night my father switched off the lights and we sat in candlelight, just waiting for the bombing to begin. Even before the war began we heard the sirens as they were testing the early warning system.

And then it all began. Unlike the 1991 war, when we could hear the planes approaching, this time we could not hear the stealth bombers. But we would know they were coming from the firing of the anti-aircraft guns, and then the explosions would sound.

I can recognize the different planes if you show me pictures.

Around the time the war began, I had gone to the stream at the back of our house with some friends. I saw two US helicopters flying around. They were probably surveying the area. I was so afraid, just seeing them. But my friends spotted the pilots and waved at them enthusiastically and the pilots waved back. So I joined in the waving.

The coalition forces or, as we called them, *quaat altahaluf*, came into our town as well. We did not see troops from other countries, only American soldiers. I remember watching them from our window and they pointed a weapon at me and I could see the green laser dancing on the window. I was fascinated but also terrified. Mama kept calling me back from the window.

There was a shelter outside and when the siren sounded people rushed to hide inside it. But Baba decided it was best we stayed together in our home. We hid inside a small pantry room away from the windows.

We watched the toppling of the massive 39-foot statue of Saddam Hussein in Firdos Square, Baghdad, on television. That was in August 2003. The American troops wrapped his face with a US flag.

At first I was happy and relieved. I thought the war would end and we would be free and safe. But Baba and Mama said Saddam was after all the president of our country and it was not right to show this kind of disrespect to him. I realized they were right, and I felt sad.

I thought the war had finally ended and at last there would be peace in Iraq. But we could not express our happiness because outside our house others were walking around with placards denouncing the American occupation. Perhaps the people were genuinely protesting against the US invasion, I cannot say.

But it was possible that they were afraid that if they did not protest Saddam Hussein would punish them; because the Americans had still not captured him and people still feared that he would rule again. Saddam Hussein declared Al Hawasim or "the decisive war". It was supposed to be the ultimate war, ending in decisive defeat of the US troops. But there was no such final victory. It was the beginning of just another nightmare in our history.

I was mistaken in thinking the defeat of Saddam Hussein would bring peace and we could begin to live normal lives. I was probably the idiot that 'Riverbend' talks about. Riverbend is a 24-year-old woman who ran a blog through those years. In 2013, reflecting on those years after a decade, she wrote: "Back in 2003, one year seemed like a lifetime ahead. The idiots said, 'Things will improve immediately.' The optimists were giving our occupiers a year, or two... The realists said,

'Things won't improve for at least five years.' And the pessimists? The pessimists said, 'It will take ten years. It will take a decade.'"

As I said, I was among those idiots who thought things would improve with the US invasion. But then I could also have been counted among the optimists who believed that things would improve in two or three years; eventually I joined the pessimists but I never saw things improve at all. I was just hoping and hoping and hoping that Iraq would become once again a prosperous country as it had been since Sumerian times.

But now, living in exile, I cannot help but hope like an "idiot" that Iraq will one day become a truly independent country and perhaps I can contribute to that process....

Let me go back to my story. Instead of a decisive victory, people began looting. There was rampant plunder of government buildings, banks, Iraqi army bases and businesses after the war. So 'hawasim' became slang for a thief or robber; groups of looters were called *al-hawasim* or gangs of looters.

Apart from the looting, some resistance did happen. Sections of Saddam Hussein's army resisted the US occupation and so the war continued. Apart from the old Iraqi army, the Mujahideen emerged soon after the fall of Baghdad to lead the resistance to the occupation. The war was prolonged far beyond what we had imagined.

The Jaish al-Mujahideen (Army of the Holy Warrior) is a Sunni militant group in Iraq which emerged in late 2004. It was a founding member of the Political Council for the Iraqi Resistance (PCIR). Although its tone was nationalist in rhetoric it was really a Sunni religious force.

Since my father worked in a defence facility we were vulnerable to being attacked by the Americans. And that made us vulnerable to attacks by the Mujahideen. Right in front of our apartment they parked a pick-up on which was mounted an anti-aircraft gun. At the time, the Mujahideen did not seem like resistance to us because they were targeting Shias—calling us traitors. For us, both the US troops and the Mujahideen constituted a scary presence.

An estimated 151,000 to 1,033,000 Iraqis died in the first three to five years of conflict.

The Americans dropped leaflets asking us to provide information on the *iirhabieen* which in Arabic means terrorist. They called the Mujahideen terrorists. They dropped small pictures the size of playing cards of Saddam Hussein and asked for information on him. Our President was eventually caught on December 13, 2003 and executed in 2006. We saw it all on television.

AKKAD

Three weeks into the invasion of Iraq, the coalition forces led by the US declared victory on April 14, 2003, just a few days before my 12th birthday.

I remember the screaming of sirens and the exploding of bombs which caused vibrations that shook our window panes. We heard the firing of the anti-aircraft guns and the blasts of bombs.

The first time I saw a Mujahideen was when my friends called me to see something very important. I ran to where they were gathered and I saw a dismembered leg. It was lying there with blood all over. We gazed at it with fascinated horror. And then we spotted a head on an electricity cable overhead and pieces of flesh and blood scattered everywhere. Then someone shouted: "Sniper!" and we next saw an American sniper standing on top of the water storage tank and we ran helter-skelter back home. I had just seen the dismembered body of a suicide warrior who had blown himself up in front of a school across from the market within our complex.

I heard that the Mujahideen were fighting the US Army. I remember American soldiers offering us chocolates in exchange for information on the Mujahideen hideouts.

BABIL

We saw some really gruesome sights on television every day. We heard that some of the worst acts of violence were committed by the Al Quwat Al Qadhura or "the dirty force". These were soldiers who wore black uniforms, not the US Army one.* Later, I learnt they were called the Blackwater mercenary army.

There was a terrible incident, known as the first Fallujah war. I saw it on television. The Mujahideen mowed down four armed Blackwater soldiers with machine gun fire and tossed a grenade through a window of their SUV. The mob that gathered then set the bodies ablaze, and the corpses were dragged through the streets before being hung over a bridge across the Euphrates.

I felt disturbed by the images and was unsure whether this was a way of winning the war; I was also concerned about how the Americans would retaliate.

Soon after, the second Fallujah war occurred in April 2004. It is considered the bloodiest battle of the entire Iraq war for American troops. It was also the first major engagement solely against Mujahideen.

By the time the third battle of Fallujah took place in 2016, Akkad and I would be far away, in India.

We felt the impact of these battles in our housing complex because the encounters between the US troops and the Mujahideen compelled the people from Fallujah

---

*Blackwater was renamed Xe Services and more recently Academi. It is the most high-profile embodiment of what is described as the outsourcing of warfare. It has in the process acquired increasing notoriety for contempt for the rule of law and violations of human rights.

to leave their homes and take refuge in our housing complex. As people poured in, they were housed in our schools and each refugee family was given one classroom.

This meant that our classes were suspended. So, for the last two years of my schooling, I could not attend classes.

I recall my final-year school examinations taking place in a large hall. I was more nervous than I had ever been during the war. Our teacher knew that we had not been able to study so he looked away even though he knew we had brought notes into the exam hall. After the examinations, the notes could be seen strewn outside the hall.

Despite the notes, I failed the Arabic examination. This meant that I had to go all the way to Fallujah to take the examination again. The road to Fallujah was blocked by the US troops. Before entering the city, we were questioned by a marine with his laptop taking our fingerprints, a scan of the eyes and a full-body scan. By the time he had finished all that I had memorized for my exam had dissipated from my brain.

Fallujah had changed so much. We used to go to a popular restaurant there, Kebab Haji Hussein. Everyone went there, even the American troops and the Mujahideen. We used to go for their famous seekh kebabs. Our seekh kebabs are very different from the Indian kebabs, much longer and with different spices.

The Americans decided Haji Hussein was an insurgents' meeting point and blasted it with a 2,000-lb. bomb. But, if the Mujahideen went there to eat kebabs, so did the Americans and the foreign journalists too.

AKKAD

I do not remember Babil going to Fallujah but I heard that Kebab Haji Hussein had opened a branch in Baghdad and that too was bombed though I am not too sure.

But I do recall the refugees from Fallujah. They kept coming. When the classrooms were filled with the refugees, they put up tents for us and our classes were held in the tents.

The children from Fallujah and we from the housing complex studied together; four students had to sit on a bench meant for two. If we complained, we were told we must be kind to the children from Fallujah who were our guests.

But these classes were of no use because there was so much noise. The people were talking, babies were crying and we were some 40 to 50 students stuffed inside one tent. We could not hear the teacher's voice. We were given books in a bag with the American flag painted on it. It was from USAID.

BABIL

I remember that the Americans gave us packets of food. I did not know the names of the things inside but there was a bag which, if we shook it very hard, became very hot and then you could heat the food. It was a bit like magic.

AKKAD

There were so many refugees coming from Fallujah that they took away the tents in which the classes were conducted to accommodate the new refugees.

In any case, everyone was promoted from the fourth class to the fifth, and then from fifth to sixth.

Some of the refugees were a rather rough set of people, they even attacked the families living inside the housing complex.

The worst was the killing of Sheikh Shawkat.

BABIL

Akkad and I went to the mosque inside our housing complex for religious instruction. Both Sunnis and Shias used to go there and there was no tension between the two communities. I loved winning prizes in competitions set by our teacher. The prizes would be pencils and notebooks or a school bag. It was near this mosque that Sheikh Shawkat Al-Ani was assassinated. He had been preaching about the importance of maintaining unity among Shias and Sunnis and, as he was on his way home, some assailants rained bullets on him and he died. Just talking of unity among Shias and Sunnis had become dangerous and could get you killed.

The US troops could be seen everywhere. Some of us would run after them shouting, "Mister, mister, chocolates." And they would give us chocolates.

The American troops came into our homes to search for weapons. They came several times but they were not aggressive and when we asked them to allow our mother to wait in a separate room, they did not enter it.

I recall an American asking in the market whether anyone knew English. He had got out of a Humvee (high-mobility, multipurpose, four-wheel drive military vehicle). The soldier wanted to know who had planted a bomb at the front gate of our complex.

AKKAD

Do you remember the bodies in the Euphrates? We used to swim there quite often but one time we saw bodies which had been eaten by fish. We pulled them out of the river and put them on the bank.

BABIL

I had completely forgotten about those bodies. It was not a pleasant sight, certainly.

We could also feel another sort of tension in the air. We were beginning to feel very uncomfortable because we were Shias. There was a family which lived opposite us. Akkad was friends with the son and his sister was in love with Akkad.

AKKAD

Though I was not interested in her.

BABIL

One day, we discovered the family had left the housing complex. They did not tell us they were leaving. Many Shia families quietly packed up and moved to safer places. Many of them were getting "quit notices" pasted on their front doors.

AKKAD

There was a man who used to deliver gas cylinders. That's all he did. And he got one of those notices. They were handwritten notes warning the family to leave or they would be killed. This man ignored the notice and he was shot dead in the market near our home.

BABIL

I do not remember the exact date but it was even before the bombing of the Al-Askari mosque, one of the holiest shrines of Shia Muslims, in 2006 after which the sectarian tensions in Iraq would escalate into a full-scale civil war.*

---

*The al-Askari Shrine in the city of Samarra was bombed on 22 February 2006. It was the US President who first stated that it was done by al Qaeda. In medieval times, Samarra was the capital of the Abbasid Caliphate and is the only remaining Islamic capital that retains its original plan, architecture and artistic relics. In 2007, UNESCO named Samarra one of its World Heritage Sites.

At the time there was no fatwa or quit notice given to Shias. That came later. In April 2013 Saad al-Durihim, a Saudi Wahhabi sheikh, posted a tweet on Twitter in which he said that jihadist fighters in Iraq should adopt a "heavy-handed" approach and kill any Shiites they could get their hands on, including children and women. This was so that the "rawafid"—a term used by Wahhabi Salafists to refer to Shias—would fear them.

But there was tension in the air and we began to feel Shias were being targeted. But Baba said there was no need to be afraid of anybody. Nobody would want to hurt us. Then one day he and Mama decided to drive to Baghdad and see her parents because they had not been in touch for some time. The phone lines had been cut off and it had not been safe to go to Baghdad.

They told me that they were leaving my little brother in my care and I was in charge of the house. They would be spending the night in Baghdad. I was thrilled.

AKKAD

I remember that day. Our parents had decided to go to Baghdad to see our mother's family. We had not been able to get news of them ever since the war.

Babil was in charge of me and he played football all day and then brought the whole team home for a meal. We had planned that his friends would spend the night at our place.

BABIL

In my memory, that day was a good day. I was in charge and so I decided to ask my friends to come to our house for the night. We would cook something and enjoy our freedom.

That morning, I played football all day and in the evening I brought the team to our apartment. We cooked something and made tea. We were enjoying ourselves when we heard the taxi outside and realized Mama and Baba had decided to return early from Baghdad. They were worried about us.

My parents did not say anything when they saw all my friends and did not embarrass me in front of them but we knew the party was over. It was already dark. I walked a part of the way with my friends and then came back home. I opened the front door to announce I was back but, just behind the door I found my parents standing with ashen faces. My father was holding a piece of paper.

He held it out to me and asked: "Did one of your friends play this prank?"

It was a handwritten note on a page torn from a notebook. It said that my father was an agent and that he must leave immediately or else he and his family would be killed.

I said: "This is not a joke. My friends would not do such a thing."

My father was still not willing to leave his job and

his home. He believed he could somehow find a way to continue living in the same place. He reported the matter to the police, who said they could do nothing to help us. My parents were still reluctant to leave.

I overheard a conversation between them. My father told my mother that he had talked to one of his close friends whose wife was Sunni. From what I overheard I understood that one of the lady's brothers was a Mujahideen. My father was still hoping we could continue as we were.

Sometimes, I wish my parents had decided to leave Iraq that day and drive to Turkey. We could all have been safe.

But then we got a second notice with another death threat. Our neighbours told us they had seen some people sticking it on our door. The notice warned us that if we did not leave, my father and the entire family would be killed. I do not remember the date but I think it was in 2005.

That day my parents did not hesitate. We packed bags and left for Baghdad.

I did not know it then that in the terminology of the UNHCR we were now "internally displaced persons". In other words, we were refugees in our own country.

2

FRANKENSTEIN IN BAGHDAD*

2005-2014

Baghdad is the capital of Iraq and the second largest city in the Arab world after Cairo. It is located along the Tigris near the ruins of the ancient Akkadian city of Babylon and the Sassanid Persian capital of Ctesiphon.

As a result of the US-led invasion, and five years of urban civil war that followed, the city became segregated along ethnic lines. The impact of comprehensive wall erection to segregate the warring urban neighbourhoods has altered the multi-ethnic and multi-religious fabric of the city and has undone the earlier rational town planning.

**Frankenstein in Baghdad* is the name of an award-winning novel in Arabic by Ahmed Saadawi. It captures the surreal atmosphere of a surreal world of pointless violence.

BABIL

By the time we reached Baghdad, it was evening. We went in our car. It was a very old car and we sold it for the price of scrap soon after. The usual way to Baghdad lay via Fallujah but since the American troops had blocked that road we went by another route. It was a track through fields which people used and the road ended at Abu Ghraib, the town which is known for the notorious prison.

On an earlier occasion, when we had gone by this route, I had seen a car with sliding doors parked opposite Abu Ghraib. I saw two men sitting in it with the sliding door open and one had something in his hand and he was wrapping some wires around it. I was curious and asked my father what the man was doing. My father told me not to look that way and he accelerated. Looking back, I think the man must have been making some kind of bomb. On our way back, I saw a crater at that spot; there must have been an explosion.

I did not really know about the prison or the horrific barbarity going on there. I learnt of it only after the tortures were exposed in 2004. We could not believe the Americans could have been involved in such acts of cruelty. We felt angry and shocked because we used to call the American troops *alquaat alsadiqa* or friendly forces.

On that day, when we were heading to Baghdad,

I remember being excited about the thought that we would be living there. I did not fully understand the implications of the notice stuck on our door except that it was something dangerous and it filled us with fear. But then we were going to Baghdad and I thought we were going to safety, to the home of my grandmother and I would be meeting my favourite cousin.

I do not remember much about our journey to Baghdad; I recall we reached my grandmother's home and everyone gathered around us and said they were relieved that we had reached safe and sound.

AKKAD

I remember the journey well. I was scared all the way. We were stopped so many times by the American troops. In a way, we felt safe because it was the US Army and not the Mujahideen but it was also not nice to be stopped and checked at checkpoints manned by the US troops.

They had a translator who asked us whether we were carrying any weapons. They flashed their torches on our faces.

When we finally reached Baghdad and arrived at my grandmother's home, I was relieved. The house had been divided between the two brothers of my mother—her elder brother and his family lived upstairs and the younger brother and his wife lived downstairs. Our grandmother had a hall and one room. She vacated her living quarters for our family, and went and lived with her elder son upstairs.

The room in which we lived was just under the staircase and we did not have access to a washroom.

BABIL

Those were really hard times. I remember my mother cooking in a kitchen outside where it was so cold that I could see her breath steaming. My parents did not eat in order to save food for us.

We could have used the washroom of my mother's younger brother's section of the house but Baba said that instead of disturbing them we could just go behind the trees. And we would take plastic bags and later dispose of them. He made it all sound like fun and we laughed at our situation.

When Baba needed to go to a washroom he went across the road to the mosque nearby where my favourite cousin had got a job as a guard. He stood guarding the mosque with a Kalashnikov in his hand.

AKKAD

I was admitted to a school nearby and I could walk there. I heard the teacher tell the other teachers that I was "Akkad from Falluja". Even in school, I was a "Shia from Falluja" which conveyed that I had lived in a Sunni-dominated area so I could not be fully trusted regarding where my loyalties lay. The atmosphere in Baghdad was full of tension and suspicion.

BABIL

Have you heard of Abu Deraa?* You must have heard of the ambulance incident, it was widely reported in the media. Abu Deraa went with a fleet of ambulances into an Adhamiyah (Sunni neighbourhood) in Baghdad near our locality, calling on all young men to come and give blood, announcing on a loud speaker that "the Shiites are killing your Sunni brothers". The young men went to the ambulances and were trapped and killed.

We heard rumours that Abu Deraa had offered his victims a choice in the manner of death—suffocation, shooting or being bludgeoned with cinder blocks. Many of the victims' bodies were found in the Al-Seddah sector of Sadr City, which was nicknamed the "Happiness Hotel". They were also found in shallow graves, many with signs of torture.

---

*Ismail Hafidh al-Lami, "Father of the Shield", also nicknamed the "Shi'ite Zarqawi"—was an Iraqi Shia militant whose men have been accused of retaliatory terrorizing and killing of Sunnis. He was reportedly killed in Baghdad after a clash with unknown armed groups on June 29, 2021. Abu Deraa operated out of Sadr City, which is also the stronghold of Shiite cleric Muqtada al-Sadr's militia, the Akkad Army. He had a reputation for his command of Shiite death squads and brutal attacks targeting Sunni Muslims and cases of mass kidnappings in broad daylight. It is believed that Abu Deraa was a refugee who came to Sadr City from the southern marshes where he had worked as a fishmonger. During the rule of the Ba'ath Party, Saddam Hussein drained the marshes and destroyed Shiite villages as punishment for their uprising after the first Gulf War—this caused many Shiites, like Abu Deraa, to move to the Sadr City slum in Baghdad.

Did you see the film *Muhammad: The Messenger of God*? In it you see the Muslims call out to the non-believers, "Qatlakum fialnaar waqqtlana fi aljana". It means "kill the non-believers so we can go to Paradise". Now Shias were calling out to Sunnis, "Qatlanan fi al Jannat waqatlahum waria Al-Seddah" (our people will go to Paradise and yours will go to Al-Seddah). Now the battle was between Shias and Sunnis.

AKKAD

I somehow managed to pass for two years but in the third year I failed. I just could not focus on my studies. There was no electricity at home and I had to study by the light of a paraffin lamp so my eyes felt the strain. There was no place where I could study in peace, our family had no money and we just lived from day to day.

I repeated the third year and passed with 75 percent marks. But I felt I needed to support my family and a friend helped me get a job as a street cleaner.

I do not remember the exact year but it must have been around 2008 that I joined an institute where they trained schoolteachers. According to Google it was called Institute of Preparation Parameters. I think it closed down.

I studied five years at the institute, from 2008 to 2011 or perhaps 2012. I wanted to learn English but they said the slot for English was already full. So my specialization was mathematics and science.

Travelling by bus, we had to go through so many

checkpoints. There were checkpoints everywhere, set up by the Americans to check if anyone was carrying weapons, but there were also false checkpoints put up by militias. Those five years, when I was going to the institute, I was filled with fear because we had to cross the Azimiya, a Sunni locality.

We were stopped at various checkpoints and asked to show our identity cards. I just prayed that the checkpoint was not set up by a Sunni militia. The situation was so bad that I dared not tell even my friends my real name because it would reveal my Shia identity.

I cannot remember how many dead bodies I saw during those days. I could tell by just looking at the bodies whether they were freshly killed or the corpses had been lying there for several days.

In the final year, we had 45 days' practical training at a school. In the class I was teaching, there was one student who sat right at the back. He did poorly in the tests. I took especial care of him and with lots of love and encouragement he improved.

When I left, the students came to say goodbye and gave me a number of gifts; some brought bottles of perfume while others gave me pens.

After graduation I could not get a job as a schoolteacher because in order to get a job you had to have money to bribe or have connections with the government or in the army. Our family did not have money or influence so there was no possibility of my getting a government job.

BABIL

How can you tell whether a person is a Shia or a Sunni?

The militia will order the person to say *salat* (namaaz). There are several differences between Shia and Sunni *salat*, including the position of the hands. Sunni Muslims fold their arms whereas Shia Muslims do not.

Another difference between Shia and Sunni *salat* is the use of the word amen. Amen is a Hebrew word and Shia scholars do not consider it *wajib* (obligatory), whereas Sunni Muslims say amen after Surah Fatiha during *salat*.

Since offering *salat* is a part of daily routine, it is difficult to fake the manner of praying even if one knows these differences. There were so many cases when a Sunni militia asked a Shia to offer *salat* and, when he was revealed as a Shia, he was shot while praying; and it happened the other way around as well. It was a surreal time in Baghdad with killing and shooting every day.

But I also have happy memories such as of the time when my friends and I went to Karbala during the Arba'een Pilgrimage. It is held at the end of the 40-day mourning period following Ashura, the religious ritual commemorating the martyrdom of the grandson of the Prophet, Husayn ibn Ali.

Saddam Hussein had banned the pilgrimage and so this was the first time people could go and there were hundreds of thousands of pilgrims. They say Arba'een is the largest annual pilgrimage in the world. The solemnity of the occasion was matched by the joy of being able to walk to Karbala.

I went with a bunch of friends and we walked from Baghdad to Karbala, which is three days' walking. I remember the huge amounts of food and the *mawkibs* or volunteers who would call out to us and invite us to eat at their stalls. The stalls were full of grilled fish, chicken, kebabs and all kinds of food we had not tasted for so long.

I enrolled for a course in management economics affiliated to Baghdad University. Even going to college was a challenge and very dangerous. I had to walk on the Tariqe al Mawt or road of death every day where people were regularly killed.

This is not to be confused with the famous Highway of Death. That was a six-lane highway between Kuwait and Iraq, officially known as Highway 80.* There are

---

*It runs from Kuwait City to the border town of Safwan in Iraq and then on to the Iraqi city of Basra. The road was used by Iraqi armoured divisions for the 1990 invasion of Kuwait. It was repaired after the first Gulf War and used by US and British forces in the initial stages of the 2003 invasion of Iraq. During the American-led invasion of Iraq, ground forces attacked retreating Iraqi military personnel attempting to leave Kuwait on the night of February 26-27, 1991, resulting in the destruction of hundreds of vehicles and the deaths of many of their occupants. Between 1,400 and 2,000 vehicles were hit or abandoned on the main Highway 80 north of Al Jahra.

many Highways of Death in Iraq. I remember walking down the Highway, it was eerie and I felt I could be attacked at any moment.

One day, I was going to my college in Baghdad and the bus stopped near the Sabah Library to pick up passengers. I was sitting right at the back. I saw a man standing at the crossroads. A black BMW drove up and stopped next to him. A man dressed in black got out and right there just riddled the man's body with bullets from top to bottom. I saw the man's now lifeless body fall and the guy in black got back into the car and then the men in it popped their heads out of the windows and fired triumphantly in the air.

Another time I was crossing the highway and had just entered my locality. Down one of the streets I saw a body with the hands tied behind the back lying in a pool of blood. The new Iraqi police were preparing to carry away the body.

AKKAD

We saw so many dead bodies those days...

I felt I must work and support my family. We could not borrow money because there was no way we could return it. My mother's brother worked with a construction company and he got me a job there as a worker. I carried cement and bricks and even learnt to lay bricks.

Later, I worked in a nursery. I did not get a lot of

money. Across the road from the nursery was a US military camp. One evening, when I was working, I saw two pick-ups stop by the camp. I was weeding and when I looked up from my work I saw bodies being transferred from one pick-up to the other. They called out to us to help them. My colleague went, I did not.

During those days Babil was also trying to study in the college. He had a really tough time and he was my hero for the way he managed to graduate.

BABIL

My mother would give me just enough money for the bus fare from home to college and back. I did not have money to pay anyone else's fare. In Iraq, if friends get on the bus together then we pay the other's fare. If two friends get into a bus, whoever gets in first pays for both. To avoid the embarrassment of not being able to pay another fare, I would get off before the college and walk the rest of the way.

I did not even go to the cafeteria because there too one person usually pays the bill and there is no question of each one paying his share.

It was very humiliating not having money and I felt ashamed in front of the girls who looked upon me as a village bumpkin even though we used to live under much better conditions in our small town. There we always had electricity but in Baghdad there were long power cuts. We would get two hours' electricity and then for six hours, none.

I have always wanted to learn English. My aunt, my mother's brother's wife, spoke English well and she worked as a translator for the US Army. I used to ask her to teach me and although she was very busy and had little time, she did give me a few lessons. She would give me small messages to translate from Arabic to English and from English to Arabic. I was also obsessed with English songs and thought I could learn English by listening to them.

One day, my uncle took me to the market to buy new clothes and I felt embarrassed because we could not afford to buy our own clothes. That day a car exploded. But I can't remember the details. It was an everyday affair.

Since we did not have money to buy new clothes I would go to Bab al Sharqi near Tahrir Square where we could buy second-hand clothes. That is where I saw vendors selling loads of electronic goods, like mobiles, TVs, computers, but they were damaged goods. And in the midst of the clothes and electronic goods the vendors also sold drugs, some tablets and also hand grenades.

People had picked up weapons abandoned by Saddam's army. The Iraqi Prime Minister* asked the

---

*Following the overthrow of the Baʿath government in 2003, the United States and its allies established the Coalition Provisional Authority (CPA) headed by a senior American diplomat. In July, the CPA appointed the 25-member Iraqi Governing Council (IGC) which approved an

people to deposit their weapons and promised to buy them from the people. But people kept their weapons and there were some who had actually picked up abandoned tanks and hidden them under their homes by digging deep pits.

My favourite cousin told me he had found one abandoned tank in a field and he and his friends had got into the tank and pressed various buttons and the tank had started moving. They were thrilled!

I remember one incident particularly because it was the day I was trying to get to my college for an exam. I was walking along a road when the police told me to walk close to the wall.

The Coalition forces had built blast walls along the main highways, which they used frequently. These walls were defensive blast walls built with concrete blocks to minimize the impact of the blasts. Later, they started building walls to protect neighbourhoods from the vigilante militias or foreign militants so the Shia and Sunni localities became segregated from each other.

When the police asked me to walk next to the wall, I did so and I could hear bullets whizzing past my

---

interim Constitution in March 2004, and a permanent Constitution was approved by a national plebiscite in October 2005. This document established Iraq as a federal state in which limited authority—over matters such as defence, foreign affairs and customs regulations—was vested in the national government. Elections for the National Assembly of Iraq were held on January 30, 2005.

ear. I found myself dodging the bullets and I turned back and went home. That is why I missed one of my exams that year.

I did manage to reach for the next exam. During the exam, I glanced back and saw one of my friends sitting back in his chair and relaxing with his paper in front of him. Afterwards, he told me he did not answer any questions, he only wrote down the lyrics of a famous song by Kadim Al Sahir.*

Unbelievably, he passed! How I wished I too had written down a song instead of struggling to answer the questions.

I studied from 2005 to 2006 but then had to discontinue my studies because I needed to earn to support my family. I returned to college in 2009 and graduated in 2012. I am able to tell you these dates because I found my college papers in my phone!

I started working with a butcher who used to sell

---

*Kadim Jabbar Al Samarai (born 1957), better known by his stage name Kadim Al Sahir, is an Iraqi singer, composer and songwriter. He has been dubbed The Caesar of Arabic songs and Iraq's Ambassador to the world. He is one of the most successful singers in the history of the Arab World with over 100 million albums sold and the highest-attended Arabic concert of all time. In 2003, according to an international poll conducted by BBC, more than half-a million people from 165 countries voted his composition Ana Wa Laila (Me and Laila), his most famous song about his love for Laila, as the sixth in the world's top 10 most popular songs of all time. He performs with an orchestra of twenty to thirty musicians on Arabic percussion, oud, qanun, nay, and a full complement of strings (violin, cello, and bass).

meat imported from India. If I recall correctly, it was beef. With the fall of Saddam Hussein, the markets were full of foreign goods; it was difficult to get Iraqi-made goods. Even the tomatoes and brinjals were imported.

I had to work hard. I had to be at the shop at 8 am. I would clean the shop and sweep the area outside. When the owner arrived, we would mince the meat and fill it into half-kg packets which we then stored in the freezer. We also sold freshly made cheeses. There was also a fridge where we kept ice-cream and I was allowed to eat the melted ice-cream.

The owner would go home after work and change his clothes. Then, with a scarf tied around his head, he would sit on a chair, holding a Kalashnikov, and guard his home.

By this time we had moved out of my grandmother's home because our family had grown. We had two small brothers now.

We moved to a half-constructed house on government land. I do not know for sure but I think my father rented the house from the owner. It did not have any windows or doors. We also had neither an electricity connection nor a water connection. But we were surrounded by fields.

Cold air used to come through the windows so Baba blocked it with plastic sheets. Day by day, he improved the condition of the house; he put in windows and doors and got an electricity connection. Baba,

Akkad and I laid a pipe over some 300 metres so that we could have running water but every other day the supply would get disconnected because farmers would accidentally drive their tractors over our pipe. We had to keep re-connecting it.

AKKAD

Since Baghdad had almost no electricity, people depended on generators owned by private individuals.

I got a job looking after a big generator; it was the back-up for several homes in the locality, not too far from our home. The other person working at the generator unit was a man called Bakr, he was a Sunni. He taught me how to look after the generator, pour in the diesel and switch it on and off. The first day I got a very bad electric shock. The generator was kept on a wooden structure and fenced off with barbed wire. Behind the generator was a room where we could sleep.

One day, I was going home and on the way I was stopped by the new Iraqi army. They asked for my identity card and I showed it to them. They told me to kneel and, despite the fact that I had shown my ID, they hit me with the butts of their rifles. I was badly beaten and very bruised when I finally got home. There was absolutely no reason why they picked on me. It just shows how mindless the violence was.

Every month, we had to collect the money from all the houses that had subscribed for the generator and we kept accounts in the cashbook. One night, around eight, there was a loud knock on the door. I thought someone had come to pay their dues. Bakr opened the door and I could see his face turn white. Then I saw the barrel of a gun and I felt cold terror.

Then a man pulled me out of the room and another man appeared. They tied my hands behind my back with rope and made me kneel with my forehead on the ground. One man held a knife at my throat. The other man, whose face was covered with a scarf, had a gun to Bakr's head. I thought I was going to die and I kept thinking of my family. They took all the money and left.

Bakr untied the rope (he had not been tied up) and called the owner to the generator. The owner came and got angry with us. He said if we could not recover the stolen money, he would not give us our wages. So I left the job.

The owner of the generator later became a leader of the Sahwa or Sons of Iraq, as it is known.*

---

*The factors leading to the improvement of the security situation in Iraq in recent years have been the subject of controversy; it is, however, acknowledged that the establishment of the Sahwa Council and Sahwa forces was a crucial factor in the reduction of violence. Sahwa represents a change in the position of Sunni tribal elements from supporting the *jihadi* insurgents to cooperating with the US troops in fighting against Al Qaeda and Shia militias. The US military unofficially armed and paid members of the armed Sahwa forces—which eventually came to number over 100,000 militiamen. Sahwa remained overwhelmingly, though not entirely, Sunni Arab, tribal and local neighbourhood-based.

BABIL

Every day there were killings and bomb explosions in the city. In May 2006 my cousin had got a job at another mosque in our neighbourhood. A motorcycle exploded very near that mosque and I was so afraid that he might have been hurt. Miraculously, he had escaped unscathed.

The explosion was near the shop where I had worked. I could not help thinking, what if I had been there? The day after the explosion I went to help in the clean-up. I picked up pieces of flesh and buried them.

This was the time when our family was going through really tough times and that is when I decided to join the Sahwa. There was an advertisement in the papers asking for trustworthy people (those who were not supporting the Jaysh al-Mahdi (or any militia) to join the Sahwa and they offered arms training and a good salary; at least it seemed like a good salary to me at the time.

When I went to register my name, the Americans looked at all our names and scrutinized their list. Then they gave a list to the Iraqi army. Their list consisted of all the people they did not consider trustworthy. I was chosen for the training.

Our lot were divided into two groups; I was in the first group but my cousin was in the second. We got into the bus and went to the training camp.

The first day we were given lectures on how to do a

cordon and search; how to search cars and interrogate to elicit information from people whose cars we stopped. The second day we were taught how to load and unload a Kalashnikov. I do not remember all the things we were taught.

One night, when we were in the American training camp, we were hungry and sneaked into the American army kitchen. Wow! We had never seen that kind of food. There were chickens, cakes and all sorts of food whose names we did not know. But we were caught and the Americans pulled up the Iraqis for allowing us to go to their kitchen. Then we were given chips and juice which we happily polished off.

I did not really enjoy the shooting lessons because it was very hot that day and the rifle felt very heavy. We were given 15 bullets each and told to shoot from different positions and I was surprised that I shot accurately. One of the Iraqi army officers asked me whether it was the first time I had done any shooting and I said of course. And I felt like a superstar when the Americans rewarded me with juice to drink; the others were not given it.

We were given certificates and Identity cards. I remember mine was signed by one Nicholas.

They took our biometrics for the ID cards. We were given uniforms of blue shirts and black pants and given meals, breakfast, lunch and dinner. We lived three or four in one khaki tent and had to keep the neighbourhood safe. To begin with, we had no arms but then the people in the locality collected arms and we had a gun or two in the tent which was for the group.

We would feel sleepy and one of us would sleep and the others would cover for him. In the beginning, the officer who was checking on us in a patrol car caught us sleeping but then we learnt to sleep without him knowing.

The best part was that we had walkie talkies. And we would joke over the walkie talkie or sing songs. One day, one of the supervisors heard us and said, please focus on your work and our friend said, "Shut up."

Whatever I earned I tried to give to my parents but my father would not accept the money and told me to keep it for my expenses. I worked for around a year and then I went back to college.

AKKAD

Since I had no job one of my uncles introduced me to a friend of his, Mustafa, who had a hair-cutting salon. Mustafa said he would teach me the job and that is how I started working as a barber. The first few days I just did cleaning and also carefully watched him cut hair. Then, one day a child came for a haircut. He was very small and that was the first time I cut anyone's hair.

I started cutting hair and the clients liked me but this made Mustafa's brother jealous. One day he shouted at me and said: "You will never make a barber." He insulted me and I felt really bad so I left Mustafa's salon.

A friend took me to another salon owned by a man called Harith. Harith's salon was in the Tunis quarter in north Baghdad. Harith used to take drugs but he was very good to me; he taught me many skills, including playing with the scissors.

But once the ISIS* entered the city, they said that cutting hair was *haram* and started killing barbers. Harith closed down his salon and then I joined Ali's salon which was next-door to Mustafa's. Now I had a chair of my own. Having a chair for a barber means he has graduated to becoming a full-fledged barber.

Then we got news of another barber's killing, very close to where we worked. That is when Ali closed his salon and I went back home.

We used to joke that even salad was *haram* because cucumbers and tomatoes were mixed together; cucumbers were male and tomatoes were female! Anything to lighten the mood and dispel fear, if only briefly.

I used to help on the farm which was across from our home. The owners were Shia and I was friendly with their two sons. I remember my friends' mother's

---

*UN and US officials generally use the acronym "ISIl", the acronym of "Islamic State in Iraq and the Levant". The group itself has not used that name since June 2014 when it declared the creation a caliphate and shortened its name to "Islamic State" (IS). But the term "Daesh" (or Da'ish) has also gained currency, both in the Middle East and further afield, and has been used as a way of challenging the legitimacy of the group due to the negative connotations of the word.

kindness and generosity. She would always give me vegetables to take home.

BABIL

Our mother used to call Akkad 'Abu Khair', a kind of Santa Claus character who comes bearing gifts.

When Daesh (ISIS) entered Baghdad, everything stopped; shops were closed and we used to just watch from our window and hear the rumours of the brutalities they committed.

My aunt, who used to teach me English, and her family had already migrated to the US before Daesh came. She used to call from America and tell us how her children remembered the time when they came to our home and I took them to the farm opposite and we played with the sheep. The children were missing Iraq.

I do not remember exactly when I suddenly got rashes. It was very painful and uncomfortable. The doctor we went to could not diagnose the disease or prescribe any medicine to relieve me. It was only when I got to India that I learnt that I had psoriasis, an autoimmune disease which had no cure. The doctors said stress could make it worse.

AKKAD

I had to get back to work because we needed money. So, after sitting two weeks at home, I went back to working at Ali's salon.

I always found time to go to the farm and chat with my friends. One of them joined the new Iraqi army and one day I learnt that he was travelling in a military helicopter and the Mujahideen blew it up. His brother lost his mental balance after that. I was devastated.

BABIL

I managed to graduate in 2012. But despite my college degree I did not get a job because of the rampant corruption. I remember a cartoon depicting the corruption: a man with a fat belly and a small man standing under his belly, seeking help, and the fat man, with binoculars, saying he cannot see any poor man.

I remember my aunt got me a job. It must be before she left for the USA. It was a job as a guard with the Red Cross. I went for the interview.

They asked what I would do if some people from one of the militia came. I said I would contact the police checkpoint which was down the road. They asked: Suppose the police checkpoint does not respond? I answered: I will contact the police headquarters. Suppose they do not respond? I said I would try to stop them by closing the door. Suppose they barge in? I said, then I would allow them in and invite them to have whatever they wanted, meat or chicken or whatever we had.

On the interview panel were two young women and an elderly man; the two women laughed at my reply but the man was not amused. I did not get the job.

My aunt said I should not make a joke of everything but I think that was the right answer because if the militias came knocking at the door there was nothing much you could do.

Then I got another job. It was through a woman friend from college. How we became friends is also a story.

She had smiled at me one day but I was too shy to speak to her. I told my friend and he led me to her in the garden. I walked behind him and told her I wondered whether she had a tablet for a headache because I was not feeling well. She said she was very sorry but she did not; the next day she brought a whole strip of tablets and gave it to me! Then I told her it was just an excuse to talk to her and I had not had a headache. Both these friends are now refugees in different parts of the world. And I am in India.

After graduation, her mother, who was a teacher, offered me a job as an exam invigilator at the Law College for a month.

I turned up at the Law College where exams were being held and was shocked to find the students were all either generals or members of Parliament. Most of these people did not have educational qualifications but they wanted to get degrees.

I was somewhat amused and gratified that these powerful people were afraid of me since I was the invigilator. But before I could take my job too seriously, the dean warned me not to check them even though I could see them cheating. He said these people were our guests so we should not embarrass them.

Many of these men gave me their phone numbers in the course of the month. And several of them promised to help me get a good job but none kept his word. If I had taken photos of them cheating I could have used it as evidence against them! Just looking at their numbers in my mobile scared me and I deleted them.

After the month was over, I went back to working at the shop in our neighbourhood market. There were two interconnected shops, the owner managed one in which he sold women and children's clothing while the shop next door was where I sold accessories such as shoes and purses.

Our father worked in a shop which was farther away, at Shar Al Naher. And a day came that began like any other day. Akkad was at his barber salon, I was at my shop and Baba had gone to work at his shop. Towards the evening, I got a call from Mama saying Baba had not come home. I immediately felt a cold terror but told her not to worry as he might have gone to meet a friend. But I knew Baba never went anywhere. He always came home from the shop. I do not remember the exact date of that day.

AKKAD

I remember the date. It was on July 27, 2014, that our father was kidnapped from the shop where he worked.

Mama called me as well. I was at the salon.

We went home and waited for him. The people at the shop where he worked had been too scared to tell us immediately when he had been taken away in a black car. Mother reported the matter to the police and her elder brother advised us to behave normally. As if that was at all possible.

BABIL

I remember my mother just standing and looking at the path by which he would come home.

Then, another day like that came all too soon. I was at the shop when my mother called and told me to take Akkad and go into hiding. Some people had come looking for us. They even knew our names.

I called a taxi and went to Ali's salon and called Akkad out. He wanted to know where we were going but I indicated to him that I did not want to talk in front of the taxi driver. He understood. We drove straight to the home of a friend. His mother was really good to us and welcomed us. They had a big house and gave us a room to stay in.

We stayed in hiding for several days. And then one day Mama told us we would be going to India. She had decided after discussing with my aunt who was in the

US. She said we would be safe there. We were put on a flight from Baghdad to Hyderabad in September 2014.

Less than two months after Akkad and I arrived in India, on November 4, 2014, a suicide bomber blew himself up at the very spot where my shop was located, the one where I had worked. More than 36 people died. Had I been there in Baghdad I would not be here to tell my story.

3

BEING A REFUGEE IN INDIA

2014 Onwards

> Delhi now belonged to everyone who lived in it, but no one belonged to Delhi.
>
> —Anupreeta Das, journalist

BABIL

After arriving in India, almost every night I dreamt I was back in Iraq with my family, with Mama and Baba. I felt the reality in which we were living was just a bad dream and I would wake up and we would all be together again.

Now, Iraq and my memories of our life there have started to fade. It seems as if it all happened decades ago. I do not remember dates, months or even years. I sometimes even forget the date on which my father was kidnapped. I am told this kind of memory loss is suffered by people who have faced trauma.

AKKAD

For me, I remember everything clearly. It feels as if my father was kidnapped just yesterday, it's all fresh in my memory. We have been in India since 2014 and life has become unbearable, especially since the pandemic began. And I feel angry that the UNHCR, which is supposed to help us, is so utterly indifferent to us, to our pain and suffering.

BABIL

I know the exact date on which we landed in India. This is because it is stamped in my passport. We took the flight from Baghdad on September 11, 2014 and landed in Hyderabad the next day.

Why did we take a flight to Hyderabad? I have no idea. All those details were decided by my mother in consultation with her brother and his wife who were in the US.

I learnt later that it was my aunt who first suggested that we go to India; she told my mother that it would be better than sending us to Turkey where there were too many refugees. My aunt said India would be cheaper and it was a tolerant society where people of many religions lived together in harmony.

Akkad and I did not know anything of these plans until the day we were handed our passports and tickets and told we were going to India. Before leaving for India, I did talk to my aunt. She assured us that India was a good place to go to. She also told me that in

India people spoke English so it would be easier for us to communicate.

She told me that in India there are many religions and people are tolerant so we would not face any problems on account of being Muslim. She told us to go to the UNHCR and get ourselves registered as refugees.

I do not know why we were sent to Hyderabad because there is no UNHCR office in the city; maybe my aunt did not know that.

I had never heard of Hyderabad and knew next to nothing about India. But I thought we were being sent away for a short time and we would be home again, with our parents. I was still hoping Baba would return, safe and sound.

I had no premonitions that we were leaving our country forever; that we would not be returning home anytime soon; and that we would never see our father again.

When we boarded the plane in Baghdad, it was my very first flight and I would otherwise have been so excited but we were both so tense and anxious that we felt no excitement at all. In fact, the moment we settled into our seats Akkad put his head on my shoulder and cried and cried until he finally fell asleep.

AKKAD

True, all I remember of the flight was that I put my head on Babil's shoulder and cried all the way until we reached Hyderabad.

BABIL

When Akkad fell asleep I quietly slipped away and went to the toilet and then I let my tears flow. I was filled with fear and grief in equal measure; and overwhelmed by the shock of the events that had occurred one after the other and led us to taking a flight to an unknown destination.

Seeing Akkad cry was heart-breaking; that day I realized I would have to be his Mama and Baba; and I would have no one to depend on, only my inner strength. I realized how difficult it had been for our parents to look after us in the midst of the wars. I wiped my tears and washed my face. I went back to my seat. I did not let Akkad know how I was feeling. From now on I would have to be strong for him, he should feel he had an elder brother who would be there for him and who could make him feel safe.

There were many Indians on the flight and I recall they gave out a strong odour. Perhaps they were migrant workers going home.

AKKAD

I did not know any English when I came to India. I also did not know anything about India, I had an image in my head of elephants with red dots on their foreheads. That image was somehow scary. I do not recall where I saw that image because I did not see any Hindi films.

BABIL

I also knew next to nothing about India.

I remember seeing Indian films. I do not remember the names of the films or where I saw them. Perhaps it was on television. But I remember one film had people dancing in the streets and a boy in love with a girl and he went to her house with a lot of his friends, singing to her. I thought I would see Indians dancing in the streets. I had seen Mowgli from *The Jungle Book* on television but I did not associate the story with India until I came here.

I remember my father's friend had gone to India and later he brought a book for my parents. It was called *Kalita and Dimna* and I recall my parents reading it and enjoying the stories. But it was only when I found the book in your* home that I learnt it was a translation of ancient Sanskrit stories called the *Panchatantra*. My parents read it in Arabic, of course.

And so we finally arrived in Hyderabad.

I remember it was the rainy season, I remember the smell in Hyderabad. It was the smell of rain falling on dust. We call the smell Rehaat Al-Traab and I love it, it reminded me briefly of home.

---

*Nandita Haksar's

AKKAD

I remember the smell of the trees. They were so different from the trees we had in Iraq. And we saw so many fruits we had never seen before. There were papayas and guavas and we saw a variety of mangoes. I had never seen so many bananas. There were handcarts full of bananas and so many different kinds of them.

BABIL

On that first day we found a hotel and I managed to book a room. I did not know English well and I found the Indian accent difficult to understand. So it was as much with gesticulation as with my broken English that we got a room. That night I did not sleep; it would be the beginning of many nights of sleeplessness. I wondered what the future had in store for us.

To begin with, it was reassuring to see Muslims in Hyderabad. But when I saw Muslim men with their beards dyed with henna and in white kurtas and short salwars above their ankles, I felt alarmed. They looked like the Salafi or Wahabbis who had just come back from the war.

Our second shock came when we ordered chai and they asked us whether we wanted it with worms! We wondered why on earth Indians had worms in their tea. The word for milk in Arabic is *dudu*, similar to *doodh*, which is Hindi for milk!

I was too scared to talk to anyone. I also could not

trust people, and thought that perhaps they would rob me. I told Akkad not to talk to anyone and warned him not to trust anyone. But he did not listen to me. He is good at talking to strangers and becoming friends with them.

It was Akkad who started a conversation with a man in the restaurant where we were eating. The man turned out to be a Sudanese and we were pleased that we could talk to him in Arabic. The Sudanese invited us to his room.

Akkad put his training as a barber to good use and offered to cut the hair of our new Sudanese friend. Our host liked the haircut so much that he got his friends to come and get their hair cut by Akkad.

But we were not entirely comfortable living with the Sudanese and we were glad to meet a fellow Iraqi one day while we were eating at a Yemeni restaurant.

The Iraqi was a student studying in Osmania University. If I recall correctly, he was from Baghdad. We did not tell him our story, about the circumstances which had forced us to leave Iraq. We did not feel it was safe to do so, but the student invited us to share his accommodation and we went to his room and stayed with him for several days.

With all this tension my psoriasis became worse. At that time I did not know the name of the disease I had. But it had started in Baghdad when, suddenly, blotches appeared all over my body and head. But I did not get any treatment for it. Now, in Hyderabad, it started to worsen and I asked the Iraqi student to guide me to a doctor.

At the doctor's, I did not know enough English to explain to her that I thought it was caused by tension. So I made the sound of bombs dropping and rocket launchers firing and with gestures tried to explain that I was coming from a war zone.

Now I realize how perplexed she must have been with my gestures and sounds! Anyway, the doctor explained that I had an auto immune disease called psoriasis and I would need to be on medication all my life, just as people with diabetes have medicine throughout their lives. The medicine she prescribed gave me relief.

All this time, we kept searching for the office of the UNHCR but no one was able to tell us its location.

AKKAD

I used to be so annoyed with the Indian people because they did not just say they did not know anything about the UNHCR. Instead, they gave us directions and sent us on a wild goose chase every day. It made me so frustrated.

We tried to Google the UNHCR but still we could not find it. Finally we discovered that there was no UNHCR office in Hyderabad and we would have to go to Delhi.

BABIL

So we took a flight from Hyderabad to Delhi and when we landed in Delhi it was already dark. We took a taxi and told the driver to take us to a hotel. He asked us the name of the hotel but I just said "hotel" because I had no idea where to go.

The taxi driver took us to a hotel in a place which we discovered was called Paharganj. I saw the taxi driver take money from the hotel owner. Obviously, he got a commission for bringing guests to the hotel. I had never seen such a thing.

We checked into that hotel and then we were too scared to go out of our room.

AKKAD

I was scared when I heard bells ringing and saw some kind of religious procession.

BABIL

In Paharganj we met an Iraqi student. We got talking to him and said we needed to rent a room. He said he too was looking for accommodation. So we agreed to share a room. After a search in many places, we found a room in Lajpat Nagar. The landlord wanted Rs 12,000 a month as rent. It was just one room with a washroom and a kitchen. I tried to bargain with him in my broken English and after two hours of hard bargaining during which we tried to explain to him our situation, he brought it down to Rs 11,000. I was really proud of myself for having managed to save one thousand rupees.

Our Iraqi friend insisted we split the rent three ways; I told him Akkad and I were one unit so it should be split into two. But he was adamant. He then insisted we split both the food and the rent. But he would buy expensive things and use the heater so the electricity bill went up. The money we had brought from Iraq was running out and so finally we said we would cook and eat separately.

AKKAD

He was despicable. Every night I dreamt that I was back home in Iraq. I continued to have that dream for many years.

BABIL

We had to search for the UNHCR office. We could not find it on Google. Again, people gave us wrong addresses. We finally found an address for the UNHCR but when we reached there we discovered it was some kind of school. It was apparently the old location of the UNHCR. There they told us to go to Vasant Vihar and, finally, we found the UNHCR office after searching for it for several weeks.

In the meantime, we had found another room in Lajpat Nagar. Next door to us were two Afghans. We were afraid of Afghans because we associated them with the Taliban and Daesh. And we were really frightened when they found out we were Muslims and wanted to know whether we were Sunni or Shia. One of the Afghans spoke Arabic. That scared us even more.

Their question reminded me of the sectarian violence going on in Iraq. I asked myself how long this question would follow me; even in India I was being asked whether I was a Sunni or Shia. We simply replied that we were Muslim.

But, to our surprise, we found our Afghan neighbours were really fun-loving people. We became friends and grew to enjoy their company. We would play games with them. One of the games consisted of one person conveying what was in his mind with gestures which his partner would have to correctly decipher [an Afghan version of dumb charades]. It was loads of fun and we would laugh and it helped to lighten the mood.

I was in awe of the UNHCR; after all, it was an office of the United Nations. We thought all our problems would be solved once we were able to contact someone there.

When Akkad and I walked into the office, we were given a form to fill. I managed to fill it, using Google translator. When we were called for our interview, they provided us with a translator.

We were soon after given recognition as refugees under the mandate of the UNHCR and handed identity cards. We were told we would have to renew them every two years. Apart from giving us the identity cards, they told us about the free English language classes they held and they said they could help us get jobs as waiters in a restaurant.

However, the UNHCR did not tell us about our rights or schemes under which we could apply for assistance and they did not give us any financial assistance. But we did not look to them for financial aid because we wanted to work and earn money for ourselves.

AKKAD

We met an Iraqi who had worked for the US Army and he told me that I reminded him of one of his American friends called Rudy so he called me Rudy. I cut his hair and we became friends. He used to bandage his hand because three of his fingers had been chopped by the Mujahideen. He returned to Iraq and we learnt that he was killed by the Mujahideen.

BABIL

We were told we should contact one Nazim at Bosco* and he would arrange for us to join English language

---

*BOSCO (BOSCO Organization for Social Concern and Operation), New Delhi is an implementing partner of UNHCR (United Nations High Commissioner for Refugees) for the Refugee Assistance Programme. It has three centres in Delhi (Bhogal, Malviya Nagar and Vikaspuri).

classes. Bosco organized cultural evenings when the refugees would perform and we watched. They also organized football matches; the Afghans had football teams but we were too few to have our own team.

They also took us out for theatre and occasionally to museums.

I remember standing at the Lajpat Nagar bus stand to catch the bus to Bhogal where the Bosco office was. There was a car park there and I saw a man collecting money for parking.

I pointed him out to Akkad and said maybe one day we too would own a garage and a parking lot and make money in the same way if we don't get resettlement. And after many years our family would come looking for us and find us but by then we would have forgotten Arabic and we would be speaking to each other in Hindi! It was just Iraqi black humour but we both laughed.

We found many things strange which are taken for granted in India. For instance, we were fascinated by the fact that everything had an MRP (maximum retail price) so we thought the prices were fixed and no one could cheat us. We had never seen MRP printed on goods before. Soon, we discovered that just because the item had an MRP it did not protect us from being cheated.

The money we had brought from Iraq had run out and now I just had to take up a job. The UNHCR helped me get a job as a waiter in a restaurant in Lajpat Nagar. The owner was an Indian, married to an Afghan woman who had converted to Hinduism. One day, I saw him drag her into the washroom where he beat her. He even invited us to his home in Gurgaon. It was posh and he was obviously very rich. He had been in Dubai.

The chef in the restaurant was very strict with me and one day I was driven to tears because of his scolding. He was a Muslim and he shouted at me because he assumed I was a Sunni. When he discovered I was Shia, I do not remember how he found out, he started treating me well.

Akkad and I would go for English classes early in the morning and come back by 11 am. I would go straight to work at the restaurant.

Akkad would go home and rest a bit and then he would come to the restaurant where I would smuggle out a plate of food for him with the help of our chef.

In the restaurant I met an Indian who gave me a tip of Rs 1,000. He lived in America and I thought maybe he could help us get resettlement. He had given me his telephone number but when I messaged he did not reply. I was always looking for an opportunity to secure resettlement but we did not ask the UNHCR because we had been warned by our aunt not to. I do not know why she had told us not to.

But we also assumed that the UNHCR would see

that staying in India permanently could never be a solution to our problem since we could not even get a residential permit or a long-term visa. Without a residential permit or a long-term visa we could not even open a bank account. Many refugees had managed to illegally get Aadhaar cards but we did not want to break Indian law.

AKKAD

When I was going for English classes in the Bosco centre, one of my teachers was a foreigner, David. I think he was from Austria. In the course of a conversation one day, I offered to cut his hair.

One Sunday, when Babil had gone to the restaurant and I was still sleeping, David turned up at our place in Malviya Nagar. Babil had left the door open so David walked in and woke me up.

I was so ashamed because I could not offer anything to eat or drink to my teacher. We literally had nothing to eat. I asked David whether he wanted his hair cut and he said yes. Our room was very small and dark so I took him up to the roof. I told him to take the extension wire and throw it down so I could plug it in. Then I took the tools of my trade and went up to the roof.

David sat down and I put a towel around him and cut his hair. He looked relaxed in the winter sun. After cutting his hair, I showed him how it looked at the back in the mirror and he said he had never had such a good cut. Then he asked whether I had eaten anything. I had not eaten since the night before but I did not tell him that; I said I had not had my breakfast. He took me out to eat anyway and I was embarrassed.

We were dependent on Babil's salary which was Rs 12,000 and the room rent was Rs 11,000. So that left us with just one thousand rupees for other expenses, including food and transport.

David took me to Subway and we had sandwiches there.

BABIL

David took me out on my birthday, January 15; he brought a cake for me and we sat inside one of the tents in the restaurant where I worked. The restaurant had enclosures in the shape of tents to give it an Arab atmosphere. That day the restaurant was closed so the owner did not mind. It was the first time I celebrated my birthday because back in Iraq we do not have birthday celebrations with cakes. Afterwards, David took us to Subway and we had sandwiches.

Akkad and I used to study English on the roof, lying on a mat.

AKKAD

Babil stopped going for the English classes because he would get too tired going for classes and then rushing to work at the restaurant.

BABIL

I finished the basic course but I did not do the advanced English course. It was just too tiring.

The restaurant where I was working did not make money and so the owner shut it down and opened another one in Malviya Nagar. So Akkad and I shifted to a room in Malviya Nagar where the room rent was Rs 5,000.

Apart from the restaurant, the owner also opened a hookah place. Akkad worked there, making the hookah with different flavours. But that also did not do well and he closed down both the restaurant and the hookah place.

I had noticed some things about India which shocked me.

I did not understand why the condition of the Muslims in India was so pathetic. I felt that, although they could practise their religion, they were not really free. They lived in really bad conditions. I was shocked by the way Indian Muslims lived.

Once I went to the Jama Masjid and found rows of people sitting outside restaurants. They were waiting for someone to come and give Rs 500 to the restaurant owner who would then feed so many people with the money. On one occasion I also gave Rs 500 to feed them.

Another thing that shocked me was the way men urinated in public. I had seen this in Hyderabad and I was disgusted both by the sight and the smell. Once, in

Hyderabad, when I saw some men urinating in public I shouted from the auto in which we were travelling. The driver told me not to shout.

Bosco was once running a campaign to make the general public aware of the need to wear condoms to prevent HIV. They organized all of us refugees to support the campaign by taking out a demonstration. We were walking in the procession, holding placards, and we passed a public toilet. We got the stench at quite a distance. I shouted, "Please use water" like a slogan and everyone laughed.

AKKAD

Indian Muslims are very different from us.

One day I went into a mosque in Malviya Nagar to use the washroom, which was filthy. When I came out, a man asked me to come in and pray. It was none of his business whether I prayed or not. I told him he could not force me to pray.

BABIL

It took us a long time to understand the laws as applicable to refugees. We had come into India legally with passports and visas unlike most refugees who had entered illegally. But our visas had expired and we needed an Indian identity document, like the Aadhaar card, because we soon found out our UNHCR identity card had no value.

So we asked the UNHCR how we could get Aadhaar cards. Without them, we were finding it difficult to rent rooms. If we went out of Delhi and tried to check into a hotel they would not accept our UNHCR card.

That was when we found out that we could probably get a residential permit or a long-term visa if we went to the office of the FRRO (Foreigners Regional Registration Office). But I did not go to the FRRO. I was scared that they would deport us even though we were refugees recognized by the UNHCR.

There was the case of the two Iraqi brothers who were also refugees recognized by the UNHCR. They were married and had children. One of the brothers had gone to the FRRO where he was told to go home and bring his brother and their families. He was told that before being given a long-term visa the FRRO would inspect his residential quarters. It was part of the procedure. So he went home and called his brother's family there as well. The FRRO personnel did indeed come and have a look around and then the police took all of them to the detention centre at Lampur. And from there they were deported to Iraq. I do not know whether the UNHCR was informed or what happened to them once they reached Iraq. That incident terrified me. I think that happened in 2017.

There was another deportation. I got to know two Palestinians and an Iraqi man who liked to dance. The Iraqi man, let's call him Ajaz, had a lot of tattoos and was a hip hop dancer. He also worked as a model.

Ajaz did not want to go back to Iraq where he could be lynched by religious extremists for having tattoos. Besides, he could not pursue his career as a dancer. So he had applied for protection from the UNHCR and his application was pending. Even before they could determine whether he could be classified as a refugee under the UNHCR mandate, the police picked him up on the grounds that his visa had expired. He tried telling them that his application was pending before the UNHCR but they deported him back to Iraq.

We heard he went mad when he returned and was just wandering around the streets. He had been in love with a woman in India and she too suffered.

If I remember correctly, Ajaz was deported sometime in 2018. There have been other cases of deportation of refugees recognized by the UNHCR. So now we live in fear that we too could be deported and the UNHCR will not be able to protect us.

I phoned the Social Legal Information Centre (SLIC) to ask them to help me get an identity card. The person I spoke to told me it was not advisable to go to the FRRO for a long-term visa because they had been deporting refugees. I do not understand why India is deporting refugees who are recognized by the UNHCR. And why the UNHCR cannot protect the refugees from deportation.

AKKAD

There was another incident. In 2018 we were in Safdarjung Enclave where we used to go to play billiards. I had friends there and we would go to the parlours where they kept these billiard tables. It was winter and I think it was on Diwali day. I saw people playing with firecrackers. I asked them whether I could join in and they said yes. We were playing with the firecrackers when some goons came out from a nearby temple and they started beating me. There was even an old man who beat me. I was bleeding and I went back to Malviya Nagar and quickly cleaned myself up and did not tell my brother what had happened. But I felt helpless because I could not get any legal protection at all.

BABIL

We really tried to work here in India. After the waiter's job, I got work as a translator for Iraqi patients who come for medical treatment to India. I believe some 80,000 Iraqis come to India every year for medical treatment.

I started doing this work with one guy, Abdo, whose father had been a diplomat and before that he had studied in India. Abdo asked me to help with the translations. So Akkad and I started to do translation.

Abdo was well off and he had his own car. At the time, Akkad and I had no jobs and we were finding it difficult to pay our rent of Rs 5,000. He promised to give me $500 a month and I began work. I think I began working in the spinal injuries hospital in Vasant Kunj and then worked at other big hospitals.

But, despite my working very hard and for long hours, Abdo did not pay me. He said he did not have the money. He lived in a hotel with his French girlfriend and seemed to be having a good life. I had been with him to the shopping malls where he bought expensive jackets. But I was too embarrassed to point out that from his lifestyle it did not seem that he was short of money.

Then Abdo employed another Iraqi as a translator but the man did not know any English. Since he was a fellow Iraqi I took him into our rented room and looked after him.

One day Abdo and he went off to Rishikesh and I was left to look after two patients. They were on different floors of a large hospital and I had to go from one to the other and it was exhausting. Besides, this work is also emotionally stressful.

When Abdo came back he said he could not pay me. And on top of that he told me he did not need my services anymore. Just like that.

AKKAD

I was really angry with Abdo because he knew how we were struggling to make two ends meet. It hurts to be betrayed by fellow Iraqis. The only reason for their behaviour that I can think of is that we are Shias. The hatred and anger has dehumanized Iraqis.

BABIL

This sectarian division and the bitterness born from the conflicts impacted our lives even when we were so far from our country. It made us suspicious of one another and mistrustful. This made me very sad.

I decided to work on my own and started translation for Iraqi patients on my own. But it was not easy because of my limited knowledge of English, especially when it came to medical terms. I had to translate medical terms which I simply did not know.

How did I learn all those complicated terms? I watched Dr House* every night with a notebook in my hand and jotted down all the medical terms and procedures. For instance, once one of my patients needed a lumbar puncture. The doctor wanted me to explain to the patient what it would mean. I had seen

**House* (also called *House, M.D.*) is an American medical drama television series that originally ran on the Fox network for eight seasons, from November 2004 to May 2012. The series's main character is Dr Gregory House (Hugh Laurie), an unconventional, misanthropic medical genius who, despite his dependence on pain medication, leads a team of diagnosticians at the fictional Princeton–Plainsboro Teaching Hospital (PPTH) in New Jersey. I read about a real life doctor in Baghdad, Dr Al Qazzaz (identity changed), in a non-fiction book, *Brothers of Baghdad* by Tara Najim (2015), one of the first accounts from an Iraqi perspective which was very like *House*.

Dr House perform a lumbar puncture so I was able to explain exactly what it would entail to my patient.

I did very well and even bought a car for Rs 50,000. Since I did not have an Aadhaar card I could not get an Indian licence. But I needed a driving licence as I knew I could get into trouble. One of the patients for whom I was translating offered to get one for me from Iraq. And that is how I got an Iraqi driving licence and I thought I could then get an international driving licence on that basis. But things turned out quite differently for me.

I had a car and I could pick up patients from the hotel and take them to the hospital. For a short period we had fun going to parties. Sometimes we were the only Arabs or white faces at the African parties. We got to them through our refugee contacts since there were many African refugees and I saw how beautifully they danced and how their music was amazing.

I was making good money so I told Akkad we could start a barber shop and I could help him set it up.

We decided to have the barber shop for Akkad in Gurgaon where a lot of Iraqis live.

AKKAD

I had been cutting hair all this time and I was able to earn quite a bit. Sometimes I would cut hair on my roof and sometimes I would go to a barber shop or even a salon in a shopping mall and ask them to allow me to use their chair and cut the hair of my client; I would give them a commission.

But my hands used to shake and sometimes I would put them inside my pocket to warm them. But many times I cut my fingers while cutting hair. Later, I went to a doctor and he said it was a symptom of anxiety.

I had a lot of clients who needed haircuts and beard trimming from the refugee community and I used to get many Arab, Sudanese and African clients. Finally we decided I should have my own salon. I talked to the owner of a hotel in Gurgaon and he rented out a room to me and also said he would take half my income.

I set up the salon with two chairs, mirrors and hair dryers. I also employed a young Indian boy as an assistant; his father had brought him and asked me to teach him to cut hair. It was hard work but I was doing well. Sometimes Babil would bring his patients or their relatives who wanted a haircut and many of the Iraqis and Sudanese would come.

Then, one day, the police suddenly turned up and asked me for my passport and visa. I told them I was a UNHCR refugee and I showed them my UNHCR identity card. The police said it was not a valid identity card and threw it back at me and it fell on the ground. The police officer shouted: "Who allowed you to open this shop? You don't have a passport, you don't have a visa and you are breaking Indian law."

I had to leave the salon with my hair cutting

implements. I left behind all my furniture and the things I had bought with so much difficulty. The Haryana police was very rough and they warned me never to come back. I had no way to defend myself or even space to speak. I realize in India a refugee has no rights; he is treated like an illegal foreigner and an illegal person has no rights.

I went home to Babil but I did not tell him that I had lost the salon. What was the point of telling him and adding to his woes and anxieties?

BABIL

I had started going to the hospitals and having my own work and since I had a car I could do my work more efficiently. It was really nice to have a car and drive down for work and be my own boss. One day, I was going to pick up the patient from the hotel and take him to the hospital when suddenly a man came before the car. I immediately stopped and took him to the nearest hospital which was Sunil Hospital, Malviya Nagar.

The man was not badly injured and the doctor told me to take him to the government hospital. So I drove towards the government hospital but he insisted on getting off and went with his brother.

I went home, shaken by the incident. At 11 pm I got a call from the dealer from whom I had bought the car. He told me to go to the police station. The dealer did not come. I went to the police station and they asked me only one question again and again: "Do you want to solve the matter?" And I said yes, of course. I did not understand how the matter could be solved. This was my first close encounter with the Indian police. Later, I realized that perhaps they wanted some money.

The police then asked me to find a surety but I said I did not have anyone to stand surety for me and the police said they would break my leg and put me in jail. Finally, they let me go after telling me they would file an FIR. And they asked me to bring the car and come the next day. I had no idea what an FIR was.

The next day I went and they confiscated the car. So now I was without a car and a case had been filed against me. I did not dare to go to the UNHCR because I was scared that they would take away my UNHCR card. But I knew I needed a lawyer. An Indian friend who used to hang around with us said his brother was a lawyer and he would help. So I asked the friend's brother to help me. He charged me quite a large sum, I do not remember exactly how much, but he got back the car. I thought the case was over.

In the meantime, the dealer had put the car in my name and I did not understand the consequences of that. The police told me that my case had been put in court and I would have to go to the court. In court, I discovered I had two cases—one on the ground floor and one on the second floor.

Although the lawyer (my Indian friend's brother) did attend in the court, he was charging a fee for every appearance and I could not afford his fees. Because I had to go to the court and the police station, I was not able to do my translation work properly and I now had no money. Akkad was depressed as his salon was gone.

One day, I went to Patiala House to get an affidavit to help one of my friends and there I met a lawyer, Bhatnagar, who offered to take up my case. He was really good to me and even invited me to his home. From then he followed up the case diligently but I found his fees very high. I did not tell him I was a refugee or about my economic condition.

I did ultimately inform the UNHCR about the case. I thought they would help me with a lawyer. I was told to contact the Social Legal Information Centre (SLIC), an NGO which works with the UNHCR and does their legal aid work.

The lawyer at SLIC told me that I should contact the Legal Aid section at the court and SLIC would advise them. I applied, and Legal Aid and they said they would get back to me but never did. SLIC told me that I should wait for their response.

More recently, I asked the Protection Officer at the UNHCR to help me by providing a lawyer since I had no money due to the pandemic and no employment. The Protection Officer gave me the name of a lawyer who phoned me and asked for the relevant documents which I sent to him. Despite promising to come to the court, he did not turn up. My cases have been going on from 2017. They have added to my feeling of uncertainty and stress.

I was also anxious about the cases because my lawyer told me that I would have to pay a fine. That got me even more worried. But then I met Mr N.D. Pancholi, a senior human rights lawyer who had met us while we were protesting outside the gate of the UNHCR. Pancholi*ji* had formed a small group called Indian Friends of Refugees and they offered to raise the money to pay the fine.

Pancholi*ji* even came to court and he and Bhatnagar have said they will sort out the cases. But what about the UNHCR, do they not have any responsibility towards me?

AKKAD

We really had a very difficult time during the lockdown and that is when we felt the UNHCR had abandoned us. We had no work and no money to pay rent. We were living in Vasant Kunj and the landlady would cut off the electricity and keep insisting on the rent when we had nothing to eat. That's when I started to hate being in India.

BABIL

We realized Aunty, as we called the landlady, was going through a tough time herself, her son died and she was facing difficulties. But what could we do? Finally, by the end of the lockdown, we told her she could have our furniture and sell it and we packed our things and left.

From that point Akkad and I slept in the homes of various friends, some refugee families, sometimes students, and once a friend whose father was a diplomat. Since his family could not return to India due to COVID restrictions, we spent a month in his home. But we did not like to accept someone's hospitality when we could not reciprocate.

The UNHCR did not give us any rations at the time but after the second lockdown they started giving us rations. Akkad and I were given rations for one person. The rations consisted of rice, dry milk, sugar (but that also stopped), soya oil and soap. They did not even give us salt.

But we did not get any financial assistance at all. Not a single rupee ever since we arrived in 2014. Some other refugees had got financial assistance on a monthly basis, some got a one-time payment. We, on our part, did not want to beg anyone for money or be financially dependent. But what could we do under these circumstances?

After COVID, I felt it was not possible to stay in India. I could not belong to India, however hard I had tried. India would not allow us to feel at home. Then we saw the agitations in India and we did not understand many of the issues but it was clearly an atmosphere in which Muslims in India did not feel safe. So how could we, Muslims from Iraq, feel safe?

AKKAD

From then onwards we decided the only solution to our problem was to get resettlement in a third country. But Iraqi refugees seemed to have been forgotten and the UNHCR priority was the resettlement of people from Afghanistan, Somalia, Congo, Eritrea and Syria. Iraqis were not on their priority list.

Driven by desperation, I decided to take my mattress, pillow and blanket and sit in protest in front of the gate of the UNHCR in Vasant Vihar. It was in the evening. I was alone. I sat outside the gate and then I saw another refugee and we started talking. We spoke in English until I discovered he was from Sudan and could speak Arabic. We both slept on the roadside that night.

But I could not sleep properly because of the mosquitoes and other insects and the next morning, when I woke up I had bird shit all over me and it had rained and my mattress was soaking.

It must have been three in the morning and my bedding was wet. I got up and wrapped the bedding with a plastic sheet left there by refugees who had been protesting before we came.

I went to the A Block market and I charged my phone. I slept on the ground inside the market and used my slippers as a pillow. I woke up around five and the rain had stopped. I went to the park near the UNHCR and sat there.

A few days later, another Sudanese joined us. Then another Sudanese came but without his family; and over the days we were joined by Afghans and a Rohingya from Myanmar.

Babil used our rations to make food for all the refugees. But after some time it became very expensive to come and go from where he was staying with an Iraqi friend.

A UNHCR officer came out and asked me, "What is your problem, why are you protesting?" I told him how the police had shut down my hair salon and thrown the UNHCR card in my face. I told him I could not even travel. I had gone to Rishikesh with a friend in his car but when we tried to check into a hotel they asked for an ID card and when I showed my UNHCR card they said they could not accept it.

The officer's response was: "Why did you go to Rishikesh?"

He seemed utterly indifferent to the fact that we were sleeping at the roadside. I told him that maybe Indians are used to seeing people sleep on the streets so they think it is normal for refugees sleep on the road.

I told him we needed Aadhaar cards and he said it was not possible for him to get us Aadhaar cards but we could get long-term visas if we went to the FRRO. I told him that two Iraqi families had gone to the FRRO for long-term visas and had been deported.

The officer said it was true, that had happened in the past, but he would come with me to the FRRO. But I said that was no guarantee that I would not be deported.

He also said I had no right to open a hair salon. I said, what about my stuff. He said he could do nothing about it.

I told him how in Hauz Khas once a policeman had asked for my visa and when I showed my UNHCR card he said it was not a valid card and slapped me. Then he asked for Rs 13,000 or else he would put me in jail. I pushed the policeman and ran and hid in a park.

The police do not know about refugee rights or respect the UNHCR.

I sat in front of the UNHCR office from August to the end of November 2021. During that time sometimes refugees came to the office and held angry protests. I joined the protests. The UNHCR security guards would call the police instead of talking to us. I was arrested five times in the course of those four months and kept at the police station.

BABIL

We want resettlement in a third country. We can't go on living like illegal aliens without any rights. Living with this level of uncertainty is causing us great psychological stress.

Every other day we hear some refugee has got resettlement in some country, from Norway to Australia. We used to get news of who is getting resettlement and who is not. One refugee from Sudan whom we called "Breaking News" would tell us. He had insider information.

We saw certain refugees being called into the UNHCR office but we were never called.

Recently, we went to the Vikaspuri centre of the UNHCR where we met other refugees. A Syrian refugee told us he had gone to the FRRO for a long-term visa and after that the police came to his house every day and kept interrogating him. He said it was not worth it to even try for a long-term visa.

We were standing in a queue to renew our UNHCR cards. One refugee asked us how long we had been in India and we asked him to first tell us how long *he* had been in India. Three years, he said and was shocked to hear we have been here seven years.

We ask in desperation, how much longer?

AKKAD

While we were sleeping outside the UNHCR office one Indian woman gave us tents to sleep in. We do not know her name but she just came and handed over the tents. Then another Indian woman came out of one of the houses near the UNHCR office and called us to give us food, but the UNHCR security guards told her not to give us food.

The guards do not allow us to use the washroom in the UNHCR office. We have to go to the public toilets in the A Block market. They take five rupees if we want to go to the toilet, five rupees for having a bath and 20 rupees if we wash clothes.

One day, two women UNHCR officials were walking past us and I heard one ask the other who we were. She was pointing at us. The other one answered: "Iranians". They do not know the difference between Iran and Iraq.

I felt really angry at the utter indifference with which the UNHCR officers looked upon us. They were there to protect us but in fact they had done precious little to protect us. For the most part, the only contact we had with them was every two years when we went to renew our UNHCR cards.

What was really frightening was that so many people recognized as refugees by the UNHCR were being deported. At first we had thought these were isolated cases but now we were seeing a pattern. I learnt about a Sudanese refugee, Abdul Rehman, who had been given UNHCR refugee status who was being held at the Lampur detention centre. The Sudanese refugees were protesting regularly and demanding his release.

BABIL

After we had been sleeping in front of the UNHCR office and demanding to meet the officers for more than four months, finally the Protection Officer came out and said that if we removed the tents and went home, the UNHCR would help to resettle us in another country where we would be safe. We told her we did not have a home to go to but we would just stay with friends and wait for her to start the resettlement process. We had been patient so far but our patience was running out.

We have still not had any news from the UNHCR and now the third wave of the deadly virus has taken over. The world is worried about the virus, refugees are not a concern.

We are a long, long way from home. And the road to normalcy is nowhere near the destination. It is endless.

AFTERWORD

> Everyone in the ordinary world is asleep. Their religion—the religion of the familiar world—is emptiness, not religion at all.
>
> —Sanai, *Hadiqa*

I (Babil) am now 34 years old. I have already lived through several wars and experienced the violence of sectarian hatred. I have also survived life as a refugee in India for eight years. It has not been easy.

I am glad we have at least recorded our story. It was a painful process to remember things which I had longed to forget. At the same time, I realize that for Iraqis this book will have little to offer. They have been through much the same experience as we have and some of them have seen much worse.

All these years, I have not had time to reflect on our experiences or to try and understand why our country has been torn by such ferocious hatred and anger. It was during the pandemic, when we could not go out, that I started reading for the first time.

What did I read? I have had no one to guide me and I just looked up books which were bestsellers. That is how I came across books by Mark Manson. I especially enjoyed *The Subtle Art of Not Giving a Fu**k* (2016) which was on the *New York Times* bestseller list. Then I read *Crime and Punishment* by Fyodor Dostoevsky which really moved me to the core. I read it in Arabic. I am reading other books by him.

But the author who helped me understand my country and my people is Ali Al-Wardi (1913–1995), the father of Iraqi sociology. Ali Al-Wardi pioneered the critique of sectarianism in the Arab world. I found so many answers to questions which I had not even been able to formulate. He has been my inspiration and a sort of mentor.

Al-Wardi studied at the American University of Beirut and later in the US before returning to Iraq. What I learnt from his works was to look for the causes of things and not to judge people or events without understanding their history. Some of his most important works are: *Psychological Insights from Modern Iraqi History; A Study into the Nature of Iraqi Society* and *The Personality of the Iraqi Individual: A Study of Iraqi Personality in Light of New Psychological Science.*

What disturbs me most is the way Iraqis living in India, so far from home, do not bond and help one another. If we could have come together in such troubled times we could have offered support to one another. Reading Al-Wardi, I began to understand why we had become so aggressive and individualistic. Ali Wardi did not live to see our country being torn apart by sectarian armed groups, breeding hate and distrust. But reading his books gave me some insight into our country's history. I think we must look for answers within our own society, and ourselves.

And now I see how India too is being torn apart along religious and sectarian lines. Delhi did not turn out to be the India of our imagination; it was not friendly and welcoming. We faced hostility, prejudice and even utter indifference.

But there were glimmers of humanity we experienced, especially when we were protesting in front of the UNHCR office—the anonymous woman who gave us a tent or the couple who provided us with food.

My brother and I have tried to preserve our humanity and keep alive our hope that one day we will find a country which will welcome us and a people who will embrace us. We want to experience a life without fear, without this terrible uncertainty and the slow passage of time and our lives amid uncertainty, anxiety and the stress of being illegal aliens.

We long to have a home, our own families, and a place where we can live with peace and security.

BABIL

January 15, 2022

Appendices

THE CAMPAIGN FOR REFUGEE RIGHTS

Nandita Haksar

From the time I first took up cases of refugees in 1990 I have been aware that refugee rights are very low on the priority of the human rights movement in India. However, if we believe that human rights are universal, inalienable and indivisible, then the rights of refugees should be a core concern for the human rights community.

REFUGEE STUDIES AND THE POLITICS OF PITY

In 1989 Human Rights Watch and J.M. Kaplan Fund published *Forced Out: The Agony of the Refugee in our Time* by Carole Kismaric. It is a large-sized book with photographs and moving testimonies of refugees from Africa, Asia and Latin America.

The text and photographs are designed to arouse pity, shock and shame rather than enlighten the reader on the deeper causes of the wars, conflicts and civil wars which forced the men, women and children to flee their countries.

Much of the refugee literature is in the same vein. It consists of either stories of the tragedies that individual refugees have faced, their resilience in facing perilous journeys and some heartwarming stories of individual refugees, the lucky ones who have got resettlement in the West.

But now the refugees have started writing their own stories. They have written about the racism and discrimination they have faced in the countries where they have been resettled. How they are expected to be grateful and their contribution to their new homes is seldom acknowledged.

Dina Nayeri, an Iranian refugee, speaks of how an American once said to her: "Awww sweetie, you must be grateful to be here." Nayeri's book *The Ungrateful Refugee: What Immigrants Never Tell You* (2019) is an excellent book which counters the patronizing narratives rooted in the politics of pity.

Behrouz Boochani is a Kurdish-Iranian journalist, human rights defender, writer and film producer. He was held in the Australian-run Manus Island detention centre in Papua New Guinea from 2013 until its closure in 2017. Behrouz used tweets, texts, phone videos, calls and emails to expose the condition of the refugees being detained by the Australian Government.

While under detention, he wrote his memoir, *No*

Friend But the Mountains: Writing from Manus Prison. The book was tapped out on a mobile phone in a series of single messages over time and translated from Persian into English by Omid Tofighian.

Refugee Studies is a discipline in its own right.

REFUGEE PROTECTION IN INDIA

India, like so many countries in Asia, is not a signatory to the UN Convention on Refugees, 1951. However, India has a record of welcoming refugees from all over the world and many have lived and worked in our country for decades.

Only a small percentage of refugees in India are under the protection of the UNHCR. And even these are not adequately protected. When I first took up refugee cases in 1990 the refugees were given a monthly stipend, but over the years the amount was reduced and ultimately now the UNHCR offers financial assistance to very few refugees. Only 2,840 of 9,000 refugees and asylum-seekers with specific needs could be supported with cash assistance, leaving many with inadequate support, according to the UNHCR annual report of 2020.

Indian courts do recognize refugees as a special category of foreigners who need legal protection. The law courts have recognized the principle of non-refoulement, or the right of the refugee not to be returned to his or her country where his or her life would be in danger or he or she is likely to be tortured, imprisoned or executed.

Even when the courts are sympathetic, there is limited relief. For instance, in a case I filed as Petitioner-in-Person, Nandita Haksar v. State of Manipur and Ors. (2021), the court allowed seven Myanmar citizens (four adults and three children) to go to Delhi and seek the protection of the UNHCR.

However, the refugees were expected to pay for their travel expenses. In this case the refugees belonged to a media house which organized the funds but most refugees would not have money to hire a lawyer or pay for their travel to Delhi where the UNHCR office is situated.

India recognizes the United Nations High Commission for Refugees (UNHCR) and there was a time when refugees protected by the UNHCR were offered minimum protection.

However, more recently the Indian authorities have been detaining and deporting even refugees protected by the UNHCR. Even if India does not have a refugee protection law, it is a party to international human rights standards which include protection of refugees' human rights.

INDIA THROUGH THE EYES OF REFUGEES

The experience of the refugees living in India has not been documented in a systematic way. However, from media reports and my interactions with refugees I can say that with some exceptions the experience has not been good.

There are no community initiatives to welcome refugees and very little sensitivity to their problems.

The African refugees face racism on a daily basis and the women are especially vulnerable to sexual assaults. The Muslim refugees are facing increasing levels of hostility and prejudice.

Now that the Indian Government has stopped giving residential permits or long-term visas to most refugees, especially to Muslim refugees, the refugee community has become economically and socially even more vulnerable. And they have been protesting and trying to make their voices heard.

MOVE TOWARDS REFUGEE PROTECTION IN INDIA

There is intense international pressure on India to pass a refugee protection law. This does not necessarily reflect concern for the refugees; a refugee protection regime in India would give the West reason for not taking any refugees for resettlement, as one of the grounds for resettlement is "lack of foreseeable alternative durable solution".

However, for the bulk of the refugees in India who would not in any case want resettlement, a legal protection is essential for daily survival.

In January 2022 the National Human Rights

Commission has taken the initiative to discuss the possibility of such a law. The Minutes of the Meeting are reproduced in the pages that follow.

Another initiative has been taken by Shashi Tharoor, Member of Parliament, who requested the Migration and Asylum project of the Ara Trust in Delhi to draft a Bill. On 18 December 2015, Tharoor successfully introduced the Asylum Bill 2015 in the Lok Sabha. The full text of the Bill is also being reproduced in the following pages so that there is a wider discussion on refugee protection in India.

Minutes of the In-House Meeting on Protection of Rights of Refugees held on 13th January, 2021 at 11:00 am

A meeting on protection of rights of refugees in India was held on 13th January, 2021 at 11:00 am in Room No. 508 under the chairmanship of Shri Bimbadhar Pradhan, Secretary General, NHRC, which was attended by all Senior Level Officers of the Commission. A representative from United Nations High Commissioner for Refugees (UNHCR), Shri Kiri Atri, also attended the meeting.

The list of participants is attached at **Annexure- I**

Discussions were focused on the following:

1. International Legal framework for protection of rights of refugees i.e. International Human Rights Laws including 'Bill of Rights' and other UN Conventions/Treaties, International Refugee Laws which include 1951 Refugee Convention and 1967 Protocol, human rights of refugees & asylum seekers covered under UDHR, etc.

2. Facts/figures in respect of forcibly displaced people worldwide - 79.5 million by the end of 2019 which include 26 million refugees, 45.7 million IDPs, 4.2 million asylum seekers and 3.6 million other displaced persons. 40% of the worldwide displaced people are children.

3. Refugee protection in India - Government of India has not yet signed the 1951 Refugee Convention and there is no domestic refugee legislation, however, it has shown interest in participating in the development of International Refugee Protection Framework. Administrative instructions have been issued by GOI from time to time which provides a framework for protection of rights of refugees in India. Further the human rights treaties signed by GOI also provide protection to the refuges.

4. The data in respect of refugees and asylum seekers in India (as on 31 Dec. 2020)

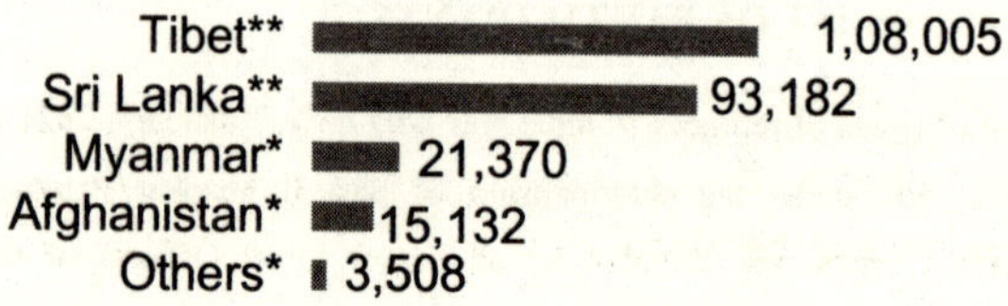

Source: Annual report of MHA (**) and UNHCR (*)

5. Way forward - Proper framework and clear policy are required to protect the basic human rights of the refugees like; education, healthcare, safe drinking water, shelter and issues such as financial or case based assistance, opening of bank accounts, due to unavailability of proper identity card etc., in this regard Commission may open a dialogue with the Government.

Action to be taken: It was directed by the chair (Shri Bimbadhar Pradhan) that the Research Division in coordination with the Law Division may work on this subject in consultation with Shri Kiri Atri, External Relations officer, UNHCR, and submit a brief report by 19th January 2021 (Tuesday) containing the steps which may be taken by NHRC for protection of basic human rights of the refugees.

Annexure- I

LIST OF PARTICIPANTS

National Human Rights Commission (NHRC)

1. Shri Bimbadhar Pradhan, Secretary General - Chair
2. Shri Surjit Dey, Registrar, (Law)
3. Shri R.K. Khandelwal, JS (A&R)
4. Smt. Anita Sinha, JS (P&T)
5. Smt. Manzil Saini, DIG (I)
6. Dr. M.D.S. Tyagi, JD(R)
7. Shri A.K. Tiwari, SO(R)
8. Mr. Masroof Anwer, JRC
9. Ms. Smriti Pandey, JRC
10. Mr. Maninder Singh, JRC
11. Ms. Prashansa Pandey, JRC

United Nations High Commissioner for Refugees (UNHCR)

1. Shri. Kiri Atri, Assistant External Relations Officer

AS INTRODUCED IN LOK SABHA

Bill No. 334 of 2015

THE ASYLUM BILL, 2015

By

DR. SHASHI THAROOR, M.P.

ARRANGEMENT OF CLAUSES

CLAUSES

(ii)

AS INTRODUCED IN LOK SABHA

Bill No. 334 of 2015

THE ASYLUM BILL, 2015

By

DR. SHASHI THAROOR, M.P.

A

BILL

to provide for the establishment of an effective system to protect refugees and asylum-seekers by means of an appropriate legal framework to determine claims for asylum and to provide for the rights and obligations flowing from such status and matters connected therewith;

WHEREAS, the Constitution of India requires all persons to be treated in a fair and just manner consistent with the guarantees of equality, fairness and due process of law;

AND WHEREAS, the Supreme Court and the High Courts in India have extended the protection of certain fundamental rights to refugees and asylum-seekers;

AND WHEREAS, India has acceded to all major international human rights instruments and demonstrated its commitment to international law and human rights norms including the right to seek asylum and the principle of non-refoulement;

AND WHEREAS, India has a long tradition and experience of providing humanitarian assistance and protection to refugees and asylum-seekers;

And Whereas, there is a need to consolidate, streamline and harmonize the varied practices, policies and standards applicable to refugees and asylum-seekers in India.

Be it enacted by Parliament in the Sixty-sixth Year of the Republic of India as follows:—

CHAPTER I

Preliminary

Short title, extent and commencement.

1. (*1*) This Act may be called the Asylum Act, 2015.

(*2*) It extends to the whole of India except the State of Jammu and Kashmir.

(*3*) It shall come into force on such date as the Central Government may, by notification in the Official Gazette, appoint.

Definitions.

2. (*1*) In this Act, unless the context otherwise requires—

(*a*) "Appellate Board" means the National Appellate Board of Asylum established under section 20;

(*b*) "applicant" means an asylum-seeker who, after entering the national territory of India, has filed an application for asylum under this Act;

(*c*) "application for asylum" means an application for the grant of asylum made under section 10;

(*d*) "asylum" means refugee status recognized in terms of this Act;

(*e*) "asylum-seeker" means a foreigner who after entering the national territory of India expresses an intention to seek a grant of asylum;

(*f*) "Chairperson" means the Chairperson of the Appellate Board appointed under section 21;

(*g*) "Chief Commissioner" means the Chief Commissioner of the Commission appointed under section 17;

(*h*) "child" means any person under the age of 18 years;

(*i*) "Commission" means the National Commission for Asylum established under section 16;

(*j*) "Commissioner" means a Commissioner of the Commission appointed under section 17;

(*k*) "country of origin" means the country of nationality of the refugee or asylum-seeker, or, if he has no nationality, the country of his former ordinary residence;

(*l*) "dependant" in relation to an asylum-seeker or a refugee, includes the spouse, any dependant child, or aged or infirm family member of such asylum-seeker or refugee;

(*m*) "foreigner" means a person who is not a citizen of India;

(*n*) "hearing" means the proceedings before the Commission or the Appellate Board, as the case may be, under the terms of this Act;

(*o*) "mass influx" means a situation where considerably large numbers of people from a specific country or geographical area, arrive at, or cross, an international border of India, and are notified as such under section 30;

(*p*) "Member" means a Member of the Appellate Board appointed under section 21 of this Act;

(*q*) "nationality" means the status of a person who is attached to a state by the tie of allegiance and includes but is not limited to citizenship, membership of an ethnic, linguistic or racial group.

(*r*) "person" does not includes any company or association or body of individuals, whether incorporated or not;

(*s*) "persons with special needs" include unaccompanied children, disabled persons, aged or infirm persons, pregnant women, single mothers or single fathers with accompanying child or children or persons who have been subjected to torture, rape or other serious psychological, physical or sexual violence;

(*t*) "prescribed" means prescribed by rules made under this Act; and

(*u*) "refugee" means an applicant whose application for asylum has been determined to meet the criteria under section 4 by the Commission or the Appellate Board, as the case may be, under the terms of this Act or who has been declared to be a refugee by a notification under section 30.

Principles of refugee protection.

3. In exercising the powers conferred by this Act, regard shall be had to the following considerations, namely—

(*a*) that all foreigners who have faced or are at risk of facing persecution in their country of origin, and who enter India, whether directly from their country of origin or indirectly, or who are already persent in India, are entitled to seek asylum;

(*b*) that care has to be taken to ensure that the principle of *non-refoulement* mentioned under section 8 is upheld;

(*c*) that the determination of applications for asylum must be by a fair and transparent system that must abide at all times with the norms of due process;

(*d*) that asylum-seekers are entitled to interim legal protection and shall not be expelled or returned before a final decision on asylum is reached;

(*e*) that asylum-seekers and refugees are vulnerable persons deserving of basic social and economic protection;

(*f*) that the repatriation of a refugee to his country of origin must be conducted in a safe and dignified manner and only after ensuring that the decision to repatriate is voluntary and informed; and

(*g*) that the unity of a refugee's family shall be maintained.

CHAPTER II

PRINCIPLES OF REFUGEE STATUS

Criteria for recognition as a refugee.

4. (*1*) A person qualifies as a refugee for the purposes of this Act if such person—

(*a*) is outside his country of origin and is unable or unwilling to return to or avail himself of the protection of that country because of a well-founded fear of persecution on account of race, religion, sex, nationality, ethnicity, membership of a particular social group or political opinion; or

(*b*) has left his country owing to serious and indiscriminate threats to life, physical integrity or freedom resulting from generalized violence or events seriously disturbing public order.

(*2*) Dependants of a person who qualifies as a refugee under sub-section (*1*) shall also be deemed to be refugees.

(*3*) In the case of a person who has more than one nationality, the term country of origin shall mean each of the countries of which he has nationality.

Exclusion.

5. (*1*) A person shall be excluded from protection under this Act if—

(*a*) there are serious reasons for considering that—

(*i*) he has committed a crime against peace, a war crime or a crime against humanity, as defined in any international legal instrument dealing with any such crimes which India has acceded to; or

(*ii*) he has committed a serious non-political crime outside India prior to his entry into the national territory; or

(*iii*) he has committed inhuman acts for any reason whatsoever outside of India; or

(*iv*) he has instigated, abetted or otherwise participated in committing the acts mentioned in sub-clauses (*i*), (*ii*) or (*iii*); or

(*b*) he poses a serious threat to the public order or national security of India and—

(*i*) has been convicted of an offence in India which is punishable by a term of imprisonment of at least 10 years; or

(*ii*) has committed an act outside India that, if committed in India, would constitute an offence punishable by a term of imprisonment of at least 10 years; or

(*c*) he has been recognised by competent authorities of India as having the rights and obligations of an Indian citizen.

(*2*) The exclusion of the applicant from protection under this Act shall not require the exclusion of his dependants where none of the reasons for exclusion applies to them.

Cessation.

6. (*1*) A person shall cease to be a refugee for the purposes of this Act if—

(*a*) he can no longer refuse to avail himself of the protection of the country of his citizenship, because the circumstances in respect to which he was recognised as a refugee have ceased to exist; or

(*b*) he voluntarily re-avails himself of the protection of his country of origin; or

(*c*) he has acquired the citizenship of India; or

(*d*) he has acquired the citizenship of some other country and enjoys the protection of that country; or

(*e*) he has voluntarily re-established himself in the country which he left, or outside which he remained owing to fear of persecution; or

(*f*) he has voluntarily regained the citizenship that he had been deprived of; or

(*g*) he, having been stateless, is able to return to the country of former ordinary residence as the circumstances in respect to which he was recognised as a refugee no longer apply.

(*2*) In the assessment under clauses (*a*) and (*g*) of sub-section (*1*),—

(*i*) consideration shall be given to whether the circumstances upon which the status was granted no longer apply or have changed significantly and permanently; and

(*ii*) due consideration shall further be given to any compelling reasons presented by the refugee concerned, arising out of previous persecution, for refusing to return to his country of origin or his former ordinary residence.

Cancellation and revocation.

7. (*1*) A person's status as a refugee may be cancelled for the purposes of this Act if—

(*a*) he, or a third party acting on his behalf, misrepresented or concealed facts that were material to the determination of refugee status, with or without fraudulent intent; or (*b*) he is guilty of misconduct, including threats or bribery; or

(*c*) there was an error of fact or law in the granting of the status; or

(*d*) there was misconduct or administrative error at any stage in the hearing, including the wrongful issuance of relevant documents.

(*2*) A person's status as a refugee shall be revoked for the purposes of this Act if he subsequently engages in conduct that falls within the exclusion criteria under section 5.

Principle of *Non-refoulement.*

8. No refugee present within the national territory of India shall be expelled or returned in any manner whatsoever to any country where his life or freedom would be threatened on account of his race, religion, sex, nationality, ethnicity, membership of a particular social group or political opinion.

Provisions for removal from India.

9. (*1*) Subject to section 8, a refugee or asylum-seeker may be removed from India only if—

(*a*) the concerned authority of the Central Government has certified that the refugee or asylum-seeker falls within the grounds specified under sub-section (*1*) of section 5, or sub-section (*1*) of section 6 or section 7; or

(*b*) his application for asylum has been finally denied.

(*2*) The removal of a person on the grounds specified in sub-section (*1*) shall be effected only after such person has been duly informed of the intention of the Central Government to remove him and given the opportunity to show cause against such removal, within such time and in such manner as may be prescribed, with regard thereto.

(*3*) Where an order is made for the removal of a refugee or asylum-seeker from India, any dependant of such refugee or asylum-seeker, who has not been granted asylum, may be included in such an order and removed from India:

Provided that before any order for the removal of a dependant is made, such dependant shall be afforded a reasonable opportunity to make an application for asylum and he either fails to apply or his application for asylum is finally denied by the Appellate Board.

(*4*) The Central Government may, by an order in writing, cause any refugee or asylum-seeker ordered to be removed from India, to be detained pending such removal.

(*5*) Where an order for removal is made, the concerned refugee or asylum-seeker will be removed to his country of origin:

Provided that where such refugee or asylum-seeker wishes to be removed to a third country, he shall be afforded reasonable time to obtain approval from such country, for his removal to that country.

(*6*) An order for removal shall be made only by the concerned authority of the Central Government in writing.

(*7*) An order for removal shall not be made until the final determination of an application for asylum under this Act.

CHAPTER III

Procedure to apply for Asylum

Application for asylum.

10. (*1*) Every asylum-seeker shall have the right to make an application for asylum addressed to the Commission in such manner as may be prescribed.

(*2*) Where a police officer or any other person exercising powers under the Foreigners
31 of 1946 Act, 1946, intercepts a foreigner who is seeking entry into India at any port of entry or international border and who expresses the intention to make an application for asylum, such

police officer or person shall not deny entry into the national territory to such asylum-seeker and shall give him the necessary information regarding the procedure for asylum, and assist him in making an application for asylum under this Act.

(*3*) An application for asylum shall be made within sixty days following the asylum-seeker's entry into India:

Provided that the Commission may extend the period for making an application for asylum if it is satisfied that the asylum-seeker was prevented for sufficient reasons from filing the application:

Provided further that the Commission may, after due consideration, admit an application for asylum after the said period of sixty days, where such application is based on a claim arising as a consequence of events which have occurred in the asylum-seeker's country of origin since his departure, or because of a significant intensification of pre-existing factors since his departure, or because of a change in his personal circumstances:

Provided also that the Commission may, after due consideration, admit a fresh application for asylum made by the asylum-seeker after the said period of sixty days, where his previous application for asylum was finally rejected, provided however that such fresh application for asylum must arise out of change in the asylum-seeker's personal circumstances or change in the circumstances in his country of origin.

(*4*) The applicant may apply on behalf of accompanying family members who are not his dependants but whose applications are on the same grounds, provided a written consent of the adult family members is attached to the application made on their behalf.

(*5*) No asylum-seeker shall be detained or subjected to any penalty solely on account of his illegal entry into, or stay in India, pending the determination of his application for asylum.

(*6*) Every applicant shall, upon submitting the application for asylum, be issued a registration document by the Commission in the prescribed form, valid for six months and containing identity information of the applicant and, where applicable, the identity information of his dependants and which shall enable those included in it to stay in India pending the determination of the application for asylum, and shall be issued without being subject to any fee:

Provided that where the decision on the application for asylum is not issued before the expiry of the registration document, the document shall be renewed for a further period of sixty days at a time, until a decision is issued.

(*7*) Where the application for asylum is rejected by the Commission, the registration document shall be renewed for a period of sixty days from the date of such decision:

Provided that where the applicant files an appeal application before the Appellate Board, the Commission shall renew the registration document as under sub-section (*2*) of section 12.

Commission to determine application for asylum.

11. (*1*) The Commission shall examine every application for asylum and, after giving an opportunity to the applicant to be heard, and after making such further inquiry as is necessary under this Act, determine whether the applicant is entitled to be recognised as a refugee in accordance with the principles under this Act.

(*2*) During the hearing under sub-section (*1*), the applicant shall be informed of and provided with the services of a competent interpreter and adequate opportunity to present evidence in support of his case.

(*3*) The Commission shall, within three months of the conclusion of the hearing, issue a decision in accordance with section 14, granting or denying asylum to the applicant.

(*4*) Where an application for asylum is accepted by the Commission, or where the appeal application is accepted by the Appellate Board, the Commission shall issue a refugee certificate containing identity information and indicating the legal status of the refugee and his dependants where applicable and which shall enable those included in it to stay in India legally.

(*5*) Where an application for asylum is rejected, the Commission shall issue a rejection letter containing detailed reasons for the decision.

Appeal to lie to the Appellate Board.

12. (*1*) An applicant aggrieved by a decision of the Commission made under this Act, may, within sixty days from the date of such decision and in such manner and form, as may be prescribed, prefer an appeal to the Appellate Board:

Provided that the Appellate Board may accept an appeal application after the stipulated time period if reasonable cause for the delay is shown.

(*2*) On receipt of an appeal application under sub-section (*1*), the Appellate Board shall direct the Commission to renew the registration document issued under sub-section (6) of section 10 for a period of sixty days at a time, until a final decision is issued.

(*3*) The appellate Board may, after giving an opportunity to the applicant to be heard, and after making such further inquiry as is necessary under this Act, confirm, modify or set aside the decision of the Commission.

(*4*) During the hearing under sub-section (*3*), the applicant shall be entitled to all the rights set out in sub-section (*2*) of section 11.

(*5*) The appellate Board shall, within three months of the conclusion of the hearing, issue a decision in accordance with section 14.

(*6*) Where an application for asylum is accepted at appeal, the Appellate Board shall direct the Commission to issue a refugee certificate as under sub-section (*4*) of section 11.

(*7*) Where an appeal application is rejected, the Appellate Board shall issue a rejection letter containing reasons for the decision.

(*8*) The decision of the Appellate Board shall be final.

Interview.

13. (*1*) All hearings by the Commission under section 11 and the Appellate Board under section 12 shall include an in-person interview with the applicant within ninety days of the receipt of the application for asylum, with a view to reaching an effective and fair decision:

Provided that where the applicant is unable to be physically present for the in-person interview, the Commission or, as the case may be, the Appellate Board, may alternative arrangements to ensure that the applicant has the opportunity to be heard.

(*2*) During the asylum interview, the applicant shall be given the opportunity to express himself in the best possible manner and upon the applicant's request, his lawyer shall be permitted to attend the interview as an observer.

(*3*) The entire hearing shall be conducted under such principles of confidentiality as may prescribed.

(*4*) Due consideration shall be given to the circumstances of persons with special needs during the entire hearing.

(*5*) All asylum hearings shall be recorded in writing.

(*6*) Where dependants are included in the application for asylum, only those above thirteen years of age shall be interviewed.

Decision to be reasoned.

14. (*1*) All decisions of the Commission and Appellate Board shall contain, in writing, the reasons for arriving at the decision, and a copy of the same shall furnished to the Applicant.

(*2*) The decisions, judgements, decrees or orders of the Commission and Appellate Board shall be published, as prescribed, with due regard to principles of confidentiality.

Right to legal representation.

15. (*1*) The applicant or refugee, as the case may be, shall have the right to seek the assistance of a legal practitioner of his choice.

(*2*) Legal assistance shall include legal representation throughout the hearing conducted by the Commission or the Appellate Board, as the case may be.

CHAPTER IV

CONSTITUTION, FUNCTIONS AND POWERS OF AUTHORITIES

Establishment of National Commission for Asylum.

16. (*1*) With effect from such date as the Central Government may, by notification in the Official Gazettee appoint, there shall be established, for the purposes of this Act, a Commission to be called the National Commission for Asylum .

(*2*) The Commission shall be a body corporate by the name aforesaid having perpetual succession and a common seal with power, subject to the provisions of this Act, to acquire, hold and dispose of property, both movable and immovable, and to contract, and shall by the said name, sue or be sued.

(*3*) The head office of the Commission shall be at New Delhi and the Central Government may direct that additional offices of the Commission be established in any other location as may be necessary.

Composition of the Commission.

17. (*1*) The Commission shall consist of a Chief Commissioner, and not less than six other Commissioners to be appointed by the Central Government.

(*2*) The Chief Commissioner shall be a person who has been a judge of a High Court and shall be appointed in consultation with the Chief Justice of India.

(*3*) The Commissioners shall be appointed by the Central Government in consultation with the Chief Commissioner and shall be persons of ability, intergrity and standing who have special knowledge and professional experience of not less than ten years in refugee law and policy, or not less than ten years of litigation experience in the field of human rights.

Functions of the Commission.

18. (*1*) The Commission shall determine:

(*a*) applications for asylum, in accordance with the principles under this Act;

(*b*) cessation of refugee status in accordance with section 6; and

(*c*) cancellation or revoacation of refugee status in accordance with section 7.

(*2*) The Commission shall issue documentation in accordance with section 10 and section 11.

(*3*) The Commission may also inquire, *suo moto* or on an application presented to it either by an asylum-seeker, refugee or by someone acting on their behalf, in respect of the following—

(*a*) the detention of an asylum-seeker; or

(*b*) any conditions or consequent orders to be passed following the determination of asylum; or

(*c*) the repatriation of a refugee; or

(*d*) any other order that may be necessary under this Act.

(*4*) The Commission shall maintain a record of the details, as prescribed, of applicants who have been granted refugee status under the terms of this Act and shall make the same periodically available to the Central Government.

(*5*) The Commission may consult agencies of the United Nations, non-governmental organizations or experts for the purposes of this Act.

(*6*) The Commission shall undertake such measures and give such directions or pass such orders as are necessary for the purpose of discharging its functions under this Act.

19. (*1*) In the discharge of its functions, the Commission shall be guided by the principles of natural justice and, subject to the other provisions of this Act and of any rules made by the Central Government, the Commission shall have the power to regulate its own procedure. Powers of the Commission.

(*2*) The Chief Commissioner and the Commissioners shall have the power to delegate to one another such powers or functions as may be prescribed.

(*3*) In particular and without prejudice to the generality of the foregoing provisions, the powers of the Commission shall include the power to determine the extent to which persons interested, or claiming to be interested, in the subject-matter of any proceeding before it may be allowed to be present or to be heard, either by themselves or by their representatives, or to examine witnesses, or otherwise take part in the proceedings:

Provided that any such procedure as may be prescribed or followed shall be guided by the principles of natural justice.

(*4*) The Commission, for the purposes of any inquiry or for any other purpose under this Act, shall have the same powers as vested in a civil court under the Code of Civil Procedure, 1908, while trying suits in respect of the following matters, namely— 5 of 1908

(*a*) summoning and enforcing the attendance of any person from any part of India and examining him on oath;

(*b*) the discovery and production of any document or other material object producible as evidence;

(*c*) the reception of evidence on affidavit;

(*d*) the requisitioning of any public record from any court or office;

(*e*) the issuing of any commission for the examination of witnesses; and

(*f*) any other matter which may be prescribed.

(*5*) The Commission may cause an inquiry to be made into the compliance of its orders or directions made in the exercise of its powers under this Act, and may impose such penalties as may be prescribed.

(*6*) The Commission, with a view to rectifying any mistake apparent from the record, shall have the power to amend any order or direction passed by it under the provisions of this Act:

Provided that the Commission shall not, while rectifying any mistake apparent from the record, amend the substantive part of such order or direction.

(*7*) The Commission may, appoint such administrative, technical, and other staff as it may consider necessary.

20. (*1*) With effect from such date as the Central Government may, by notification in the Official Gazette appoint, there shall be established, for the purposes of this Act, a body to be called the National Appellate Board for Asylum. Establishment of the Appellate Board.

(*2*) The Appellate Board shall be a body corporate by the name aforesaid having perpetual succession and common seal with power, subject to the provisions of this Act, to acquire, hold and dispose of property, both movable and immovable, and to contract, and shall, by the said name, sue or be sued.

(*3*) The office of the Appellate Board shall be at New Delhi or such other location as directed by the Central Government.

Composition of the Appellate Board.

21. (*1*) The Appellate Board shall consist of a Chairperson, and not less than four other Members to be appointed by the Central Government.

(*2*) The Chairperson shall be a person who has been a judge of the Supreme Court and shall be appointed in consultation with the Chief Justice of India.

(*3*) A Member shall be appointed by the Central Government in consultation with the Chairperson and shall be a person who has been a judge of a High Court, or has had at least five years of experience as a Commissioner, or has special knowledge of and professional experience of not less than fifteen years in, refugee law and policy.

Functions of the Appellate Board.

22. (*1*) The Appellate Board may, *suo moto* or on the presentation of an appeal application, examine, confirm, modify or set aside any decision, direction, judgment, decree or order of the Commission.

(*2*) The Appellate Board may also inquire on an appeal application presented to it either by an asylum-seeker or by someone acting on his behalf, in respect of any decision or order given by the Commission under sub-section (*3*) of section 19.

(*3*) The Appellate Board shall direct the Commission to issue documentation in accordance with section 12.

(*4*) The Appellate Board may consult agencies of the United Nations, non-governmental organizations or experts for the purposes of this Act.

(*5*) The Appellate Board shall undertake such measures and give such directions or pass such orders as are necessary, for the purpose of discharging its functions under this Act.

(*6*) Subject to the provisions of the Rules, the Appellate Board shall have the power to review any decision, judgment, decree or order made by it.

Powers of the Appellate Board.

23. (*1*) In the discharge of its functions, the Appellate Board shall be guided by the principles of natural justice and, subject to the other provisions of this Act and any rules made by the Central Government, the Appellate Board shall have the power to regulate its own procedures.

(*2*) The Chairperson and the Members of the Appellate Board shall have the power to delegate to one another such powers or functions as may be prescribed.

(*3*) In particular and without prejudice to the generality of the foregoing provisions, the powers of the Appellate Board shall include the power to determine the extent to which persons interested, or claiming to be interested, in the subject-matter of any proceeding before it may be allowed to be present or to be heard, either by themselves or by their representatives, or to examine witnesses or otherwise take part in the hearing:

Provided that any such procedure as may be prescribed or followed shall be guided by the principles of natural justice.

(*4*) The Appellate Board, for the purposes of any inquiry or for any other purpose under this Act, shall have the same powers as vested in a civil court under the Code of Civil Procedure, 1908, while trying suits in respect of the following matters, namely— 5 of 1908

(*a*) summoning and enforcing the attendance of any person from any part of India and examining him on oath;

(*b*) the discovery and production of any document or other material object producible as evidence;

(*c*) the reception of evidence on affidavit;

(*d*) the requisitioning of any public record from any court or office;

(*e*) the issuing of any commission for the examination of witnesses; and

(*f*) any other matter which may be prescribed.

(*5*) The Appellate Board may cause an inquiry to be made into the compliance of its orders or directions made in the exercise of its powers under the Act and impose such penalties as prescribed.

(*6*) The Appellate Board, with a view to rectifying any mistake apparent from the record, shall have the power to amend any order or direction passed by it under the provisions of this Act:

Provided that the Appellate Board shall not, while rectifying any mistake apparent from the record, amend the substantive part of such order or direction.

(*7*) The Appellate Board may, appoint such administrative, technical, and other staff as it may consider necessary.

Term of Office, Conditions of Service, etc. of the Chief Commissioner, Commissioners Chairperson and the Members.

24. (*1*) At the time of appointing the Chief Commissioner, Commissioner, Chairperson or Member, the Central Government shall satisfy itself that such person does not and will not have any financial or other interest as is likely to affect prejudicially his functions as such Chief Commissioner, Commissioner, Chairperson or Member.

(*2*) The Chief Commissioner, Commissioner, Chairperson or Member shall hold office for a term of five years from the date on which he enters his office and shall eligible for reappointment for a further term of five years:

Provided that no person shall hold office after he has attained the age of seventy years.

(*3*) Notwithstanding anything contained in sub-section (*2*), the Chief Commissioner, Commissioner, Chairperson or Member may—

(*a*) by notice in writing under his hand and addressed to the concerned authority of the Central Government, resign from his office at any time; or

(*b*) be removed from office in accordance with the provisions of section.

(*4*) A vacancy caused by the resignation or removal of the Chief Commissioner, Commissioner, Chairperson or Member under sub-section (*3*) shall be filled by fresh appointment.

(*5*) In the event of a vacancy in the post of the Chief Commissioner or Chairperson, one of the Commissioners or as the case may be, Members, as the Central Government may by notification authorize in this behalf, shall act as the Chief Commissioner or Chairperson, till such date on which a new Chief Commissioner or Chairperson, appointed in accordance with the provisions of this Act, enters office.

(*6*) When the Chief Commissioner or Chairperson is unable to discharge his functions owing to absence, illness or any other cause, such one of the Commissioners or as the case may be, Members, as the Chief Commissioner or Chairperson may authorize in writing in this behalf, shall discharge the functions of the Chief Commissioner or Chairperson, till such date on which the Chief Commissioner or Chairperson resumes his duties.

(*7*) The salaries and allowances payable to, and the other terms and conditions of service of, the Chief Commissioner, Commissioner, Chairperson and Member shall be such as may be prescribed:

Provided that neither the salary and allowances nor the other terms and conditions of service of the Chief Commissioner, Commissioner, Chairperson or Member shall be varied to his disadvantage after his appointment.

(*8*) The Chief Commissioner or Commissioner, upon ceasing to hold such office, shall not hold any appointment under the Central Government or under any State Government for a period of two years from the date on which he ceases to hold such office, except where he is appointed to the Appellate Board, subject to the provisions of this Act.

(9) A Member, upon ceasing to hold such office, shall not hold any appointment under the Central Government or under any State Government for a period of two years from the date on which he ceases to hold such office, except where he is appointed Chairperson, subject to the provisions of this Act.

(*10*) The Chairperson, upon ceasing to hold such office, shall not hold any further appointment under the Central Government or under any State Government.

Removal of the Chief Commissioner, Commissioner, Chairperson and Member from Office.

25. (*1*) The Central Government may remove from office a Chief Commissioner, Commissioner, Chairperson or Member, who—

(*a*) is adjudged an insolvent; or

(*b*) engages during his term of office in any paid employment outside the duties of his office; or

(*c*) is unfit to continue in office by reason of infirmity of mind or body; or

(*d*) is of unsound mind and stands so declared by a competent court; or

(*e*) is convicted for an offence which in the opinion of the Central Government involves moral turpitude; or

(*f*) has acquired such financial or other interest as is likely to affect prejudicially the functions of his office; or

(*g*) has so abused his position as to render his continuance in office prejudicial to the public interest.

(2) Notwithstanding anything contained in sub-section (*1*), neither the Chief Commissioner or Commissioner, nor the Chairperson or Member shall be removed from office on the grounds specified in clause (*f*) or clause (*g*) of that sub-section unless the Supreme Court, on a reference being made to it in this behalf by the Central Government, has, on an inquiry held by it in accordance with such procedure as it may be specified in this behalf, has reported that the concerned Chief Commissioner, Commissioner, Chairperson or Member ought, on such grounds, to be removed.

Secretary, Officers and Other Employees of Commission or Appellate Board.

26. (*1*) The Central Government shall appoint a Secretary to the Commission and a Secretary (by whatever name called) to the Appellate Board to exercise and perform, under the control of the Commission or, as the case may be, Appellate Board, such powers and duties as may be prescribed or as may be specified by the Commission or Appellate Board.

(*2*) The Secretary to the Commission or the Appellate Board, as the case may be, shall have the powers of general superintendence, direction and control in respect of all administrative matters of the Commission or Appellate Board:

Provided that the Secretary to the Commission or the Appellate Board may delegate such of his powers, as he may think fit, to any other officer of the Commission or the Appellate Board.

(*3*) The salaries and allowances payable to, and the conditions of service of, the Secretary and other officers and employees of the Commission and the Appellate Board shall be such as may be prescribed.

Vacancies, etc. not to invalidate proceedings of the Commission and the Appellate Board.

27. No act or proceeding of the Commission, or, as the case may be, the Appellate Board, shall be questioned on the ground merely of the existence of any vacancy or defect in the appointment of the Chief Commissioner, Commissioner, Chairperson or Member, or any defect in the appointment of a person acting as the Chief Commissioner, Commissioner or Member.

Chief Commissioner, Commissioners, Chaiperson and Members to be Public Servants.

28. The Chief Commissioner, Commissioners, Chairperson, Members and other permanent staff of the Commission and the Appellate Board shall be deemed to be public
45 of 1860 servants within the meaning of section 21 of the Indian Penal Code, 1860.

Proceedings before Commission or Appellate Board to be Judicial Proceedings.

29. The Commission and the Appellate Board shall be deemed to be a civil court for the
2 of 1974 purposes of section 195 and Chapter XXVI of the Code of Criminal Procedure, 1973 and every proceeding before the Commission or the Appellate Board shall be deemed to be a judicial proceeding within the meaning of sections 193 and 228, and for the purposes of
45 of 1860 section 196, of the Indian Penal Code, 1860.

CHAPTER V

Mass Influx Situations

Powers of the Central Government with respect to mass influx situations.

30. (*1*) The Central Government may, by notification in the Official Gazette, declare such group or category of persons in a mass influx to be refugees as defined under clause (o) of section 2.

(*2*) The Persons who have crossed an international border as part of a mass influx but are not declared to be refugees by a notification of the Central Government under sub-section (*1*) shall be allowed to make an application for asylum under section 10 of this Act.

Registration of mass influx refugees.

31. (*1*) The Central Government may cause all mass influx refugees notified under section 30 to register their names in such form and manner as may be prescribed.

(*2*) A refugee who has registered his name in accordance with sub-section (*1*) shall be issued an identity card in such form and manner as may be prescribed, which shall entitle him to all of the rights set out in section 36.

Special provisions with regard to movement, etc.

32. (*1*) The Central Government may, by order, impose reasonable restrictions on the movement or location of mass influx refugees:

Provided that nothing in this sub-section shall impair the right of a refugee to seek and enter employment outside the designated area in such manner as may be prescribed.

(*2*) The Central Government may, by order in writing, cause any refugee found violating the restrictions imposed under sub-section (*1*) to be detained.

(*3*) Nothing in this section shall apply to any refugee who has been granted asylum in India following an application for asylum made under section 10.

Modification of a mass influx situation.

33. (*1*) The Central Government may, by notification in the Official Gazette, extend, alter, substitute or withdraw a notification concerning mass influx refugees made under section 30:

Provided that such extension, alteration, substitution or withdrawal shall apply only to asylum-seekers arriving after the date of notification.

(*2*) Any action revoking or altering the grant of refugee status to mass influx refugees shall be reviewed by the Commission.

CHAPTER VI

Provisions Related to Voluntary Repatriation

Provisions for voluntary repatriation.

34. (*1*) Subject to the provisions of this Act, the Central Government may repatriate refugees to their country of origin.

(*2*) The Central Government shall carry out any voluntary repatriation activities in cooperation with international organisations, public institutions and agencies, and civil society organisations.

(*3*) A refugee who wishes to be voluntarily repatriated to his country of origin shall make a written application to the Commission in such form and manner as may be prescribed.

(*4*) No refugee may be repatriated unless the Commission is satisfied, after conducting an inquiry, that the written application for repatriation is voluntary and genuine, and that repatriation to the country of origin is possible in a safe and dignified manner.

(*5*) Any order of repatriation by the Central Government shall be placed before the Commission for its information, and for such further orders or directions as may be necessary.

(*6*) No order of repatriation of the Central Government shall be implemented unless it has received the approval of the Commission.

CHAPTER VII

RIGHTS AND DUTIES OF REFUGEES AND ASYLUM-SEEKERS

Protection and general rights of refugees.

35. (*1*) A refugee whose grant of asylum was made in pursuance of an application for asylum under section 10 shall be entitlted to—

(*a*) a formal written recognition of asylum, in such form and manner as may be prescribed under section 11 and section 12 that constitutes an enforceable basis for his continued residence in India;

(*b*) an identify document of the nature described in section 37;

(*c*) a travel document of the nature described in section 37;

(*d*) apply for a residence permit and other government documents for which he may be eligible on the strength of the documents specified in clause (*a*) of this sub-section;

(*e*) freedom from discrimination on the basis of race, religion, sex, nationality, ethnicity, place of birth or any of them;

(*f*) fair and just treatment in accordance with due process and procedure established by law;

(*g*) choose his place of residence and move freely within the territory of India, subject to any reasonable restrictions that may be imposed in the public interest;

(*h*) seek and enter employment in the private sector;

(*i*) the same healthcare rights and services that apply to Indian citizens;

(*j*) free and compulsory primary education; and

(*k*) the right to move relevant courts of law by appropriate proceedings for the enforcement of rights conferred by Part III of the Constitution.

(2) Every refugee and asylum-seeker shall be bound by the laws of India.

Rights of asylum-seekers and mass influx refugees.

36. (*1*) An asylum-seeker whose application for asylum under section 10 is pending, or a mas influx refugee notified under section 30 of this Act, shall be entitled to—

(*a*) a temporary identity document that constitutes an enforceable basis for his continued presence in India;

(*b*) seek and enter employment in accordance with government policy;

(*c*) the same healthcare rights and services that apply to Indian citizens;

(*d*) free and compulsory primary education;

(*e*) freedom from discrimination on the basis of race, religion, sex, nationality, ethnicity, place of birth or any of them; and

(*f*) the right to move relevant courts of law by appropriate proceedings for the enforcement of rights conferred by this Act and Part III of the Constitution.

(*2*) The rights and benefits extended to refugees and asylum-seekers shall not be construed to provide more rights and benefits than those accorded to citizens.

Identity and travel documents.

37. (*1*) All refugees and asylum-seekers shall be entitled to a legally enforceable document of identity issued by the Central Government which shall mention—

(*a*) the identity number of the holder, issued in the prescribed manner;

(*b*) the holder's legal status in India;

(*c*) the holder's surname, forename(s), sex, date of birth, and place or country where he was born;

(*d*) the country of which the holders is a citizen, if any; and

(*e*) a recent photograph of the holder.

(*2*) The document of identity shall be valid for a period of five years and may be renewed for period as may be prescribed.

(*3*) Such document of identity shall bear the seal of the Government authority that issues it.

(*4*) A refugee whose grant of asylum was made in pursuance of an application for asylum under section 10 shall be entitled to a legally enforceable document authorising his travel from and to India, subject to such restrictions as may be specified in this regard by the Central Government.

CHAPTER VIII

TECHNICAL ASSISTANCE

Technical Assistance.

38. The Central Government, the Commission or the Appellate Board, as the case may be, may seek the good offices of the United Nations or other relevant agencies for its expertise, technical assistance and guidance in relation to any matter arising under this Act.

CHAPTER IX

FINANCE, AUDIT AND ANNUAL REPORT

Grants by the Central Government.

39. (*1*) The Central Government, shall after due appropriation made by Parliament, by law in this behalf, pay to the Commission and the Appellate Board, by way of grants, such sums of money as the Central Government may think fit for being utilised for the purposes of this Act.

(*2*) The Commission and the Appellate Board may spend such sums as it thinks fit for performing the functions under this Act, and such sums shall be treated as expenditure payable out of the grants referred to in sub-section (*1*).

Accounts and Audit.

40. (*1*) The Commission and the Appellate Board shall maintain proper accounts and othe relevant records, and prepare an annual statement of accounts, in such form as may be prescribed by the Central Government in consultation with the Comptroller and Auditor-General of India.

(*2*) The Accounts of the Commission and the Appellate Board shall be audited by the Comptroller and Auditor-General at such intervals as may be specified by him and any expenditure incurred in connection with such audit shall be payable by the Commission and the Appellate Board to the Comptroller and Auditor-General.

(*3*) The Comptroller and Auditor-General or any person appointed by him in connection with the audit of the accounts of the Commission and the Appellate Board under this Act, shall have the same rights, privileges, and authority in connection with such audit, as the Comptroller and Auditor-General generally has in connection with the audit of Central Government accounts:

Provided further that the Comptroller and Auditor-General shall, in particular, have the right to demand the production of books, accounts, connected vouchers and other documents and papers, and to inspect any of the offices of the Commission and the Appellate Board.

(*4*) The accounts of the Commission and the Appellate Board, as certified by the Comptroller and Auditor-General or any other person appointed by him in this behalf, together with the audit report thereon, shall be forwarded annually to the Central Government by the Commission and the Appellate Board.

(*5*) The Central Government shall cause the audit report forwarded under sub-section (*4*) to be laid before each House of Parliament as soon as may be after it is received.

Annual Report.

41. (*1*) The Commission and the Appellate Board shall prepare, once in every year, in such form and at such time as may be prescribed, an annual report giving a full account of its activities during the previous year, copies of which shall be forwarded to the Central Government.

(*2*) A copy of the report received under sub-section (*1*) shall be laid, as soon as may be after it is received, before each House of Parliament.

CHAPTER X

Miscellaneous

Power to make Rules.

42. (*1*) The Central Government may, by notification in the Official Gazette, make rules for carrying out the purposes of the Act.

(*2*) In particular, and without prejudice to the generality of the foregoing provision, such rules may provide for—

(*a*) the procedure for removing a refugee or asylum-seeker from India under section 9;

(*b*) the detention of refugees or asylum-seekers;

(*c*) the procedure regarding an application for asylum, subject to the provisions contained under this Act;

(*d*) the salaries and allowances and other terms and conditions of service of the Chief Commissioner, Commissioners, Chairperson, and Members under section 24;

(*e*) the salaries and allowances and other terms and conditions of service of the Secretary and other staff for the Commission and Appellate Board under section 26;

(*f*) the reception and registration of mass influx refugees, and all other matters connected to the management of such refugees;

(*g*) the procedure for voluntary repatriation of refugees;

(*h*) the enforcement of the rights and duties of refugees and asylum seekers; and

(*i*) the effective implementation of this Act.

(*3*) Every rule made under this Act shall be laid, as soon as may be after it is made, before each House of Parliament, while it is in session, for a total period of thirty days which may be comprised in one session or in two or more successive sessions, and if, before the expiry of the session immediately following the session or the successive sessions aforesaid, both Houses agree in making any modification in the rule of both the Houses agree that the rule should not be made, the rules shall thereafter have effect only in such modified form or be of no effect, as the case may be; so, however, that any such modification or annulment shall be without prejudice to the validity of anything previously done under that rule.

Empowerment of Concerned Authorities.

43. The Central Government may by order empower the concerned authorities to assist and cooperate with the Commission and the Appellate Board for the enforcement of this Act.

Bar of Jurisdiction.

44. On and from the appointed day, no court or authority shall have, or be entitled to exercise, any jurisdiction, powers or authority in relation to matters specified in this Act, except the Supreme Court and a High Court exercising powers under articles 32, 226 and 227 of the Constitution.

Protection of action taken in good faith.

45. No suit or other legal proceeding shall lie against the Central Government, State Government, Commission, Appellate Board or any person acting under the direction either of the Central Government, State Government, Commission or Appellate Board in respect of anything which is, in good faith, done or intended to be done, in pursuance of this Act or of any rules or any order made thereunder.

Act to have overriding effect.

46. The provisions of this Act shall have effect not withstanding anything inconsistent therewith contained in any other law for the time being in force.

STATEMENT OF OBJECTS AND REASONS

The recent refugee crisis in Europe has forced the world to stop and notice the precarious and inhumane conditions of Syrian refugees. This is a moment for all countries, including India, to re-examine their current response and preparedness to deal with refugees and situations of mass movements.

India hosts more than two lakhs refugees and is at the centre of refugee movements in the South Asian region. India has been a home to refugees from Tibet, Bangladesh, Sri Lanka, Afghanistan, and Myanmar, as well as to Nepalese fleeing civil war. It had also hosted the largest ever refugee crisis in human history when ten million fled persecution and genocide by the Pakistan Army in East Bengal in 1971. Despite this, India is neither a signatory to the 1951 UN Convention relating to the status of Refugees nor does it have a domestic asylum framework. However, India's practice has been to adopt a humanitarian approach towards refugees under the terms of the Universal Declaration of Human Rights (UDHR) and the International Covenant on Civil and Political Rights (ICCPR). Our country implements a refugee protection framework which is based on a combined series of executive policies.

The judiciary has also accorded constitutional protection to refugees in its judgment in *National Human Rights Commission vs State of Arunachal Pradesh & Anr.* in 1996. The Supreme Court held that the fundamental right to equality under article 14 and the right to life and personal liberty under article 21 extends to all foreigners, including refugees. Apart from protection under the Constitution, refugees also receive support from a body of complementary law and practice such as the Right to Education Act, 2009 (RTE) and health services.

The Government of India relies on the Foreigners Act, 1946 and the Registration of Foreigners Act, 1939 to govern the entry, stay, and exit of all refugees. However, these legislation treat refugees as foreigners and fail to take into account their special status on humanitarian grounds or under international law. They are not equipped to support the country's need to deal with asylum seekers and migration movements.

As a member of the Executive Committee of the United Nations High Commissioner for Refugee (UNHCR), India is committed to protect refugees and has also offered its assistance to refugees from Syria, Myanmar, and Afghanistan. Therefore, it has become increasingly important to enact a structured framework to establish a clear and consistent regime. The current global crisis clearly demonstrates that the lack of a legal framework does not so much deter refugees in the face of a crisis as leaves the host country ill-equipped to deal with the inflow. Even the National Human Rights Commission (NHRC) has under scored the need for enacting such a domestic legislation. It is important to mention that in 1997 India had drafted a model law on refugees under the guidance of Justice P.N. Bhagwati, the former Chief Justice of India, but it was not enacted. In addition it is a glaring anomaly that India is the only significant member of the UN without a refugee law, that too at a time when it is seeking recognition as a responsible international power through a permanent seat at the UN.

The proposed Bill seeks to incorporate the current policy on refugees, the principles of the Constitution, and India's international obligations. The provisions of the Bill provide clarity and uniformity on the recognition of asylum seekers as refugees and their rights in the country. It also seeks to end a system of ambiguity and arbitrariness which, too often, results in injustice to a highly vulnerable populace. The Bill proposes to enable the Government to manage refugees with more accountability and order, while balancing humanitarian concerns and security interests of the State.

India has been, and continues to be, a generous host to several persecuted communities, doing more than many countries who are signatories to the UN Refugee Convention, 1951. The Bill, if enacted, will put India at the forefront of asylum management in the world. It will finally recognise India's long-standing and continuing commitment to humanitarian and democratic values while dealing with refugees.

Hence this Bill.

NEW DELHI;
November 13, 2015.

SHASHI THAROOR

FINANCIAL MEMORANDUM

Clause 16 of the Bill provides for the establishment of the National Commission for Asylum. Sub-clause 3 provides that the head office of the Commissions shall be at New Delhi and enables the Commission to establish offices at other places in India.

Clause 17 provides appointment of a Chief Commissioner and six other Commissioners in the Commission. Clause 19 provides for appointment of administrative, technical and other staff to the Commission. Clause 20 provides for the establishment of the National Appellate Board for Asylum.

Clause 21 provides that the Appellate Board shall consist of a Chairperson, and not less than four other Members to be appointed by the Central Government. Clause 23 provides for appointment of administrative, technical and other staff to the Appellate Board.

Clause 24 provides that the salaries and allowances payable to the Chief Commissioner, Commissioners, Chairperson, and Members shall be prescribed by the Central Government.

Clause 26 provides for the appointment of a Secretary to the Commission and a Secretary to the Appellate Board to exercise the powers of general superintendence, direction and control in respect of all administrative matters of the Commission or Appellate Board. It also provides for salaries and allowances payable to the secretary and other officers and employees of the Commission and the Appellate Board shall be such as may be prescribed by the Central Government.

Clause 35 provides that same healthcare rights which apply to Indian citizens and service and free and compulsory primary education shall be provided to the refugee who has been granted asylum. Clause 36 provides that same healthcare rights and services as applicable to Indian citizens and free and compulsory primary education shall be provided to asylum-seekers and mass influx refugees.

Clause 39 provides that the Central Government shall provides grants of sums of money to the Commission and Appellate Board for carrying out the purposes of this Act.

The Bill, therefore, if enacted would involve expenditure from the Consolidated Fund of India. It is estimated that a recurring expenditure of about rupees fifty crore per annum would be involve from the Consolidated Fund of India.

A non-recurring expenditure of about rupees twenty crore is also likely to involve.

20

MEMORANDUM REGARDING DELEGATED LEGISLATION

Clause 42 of the Bill empowers the Central Government to make rules for carrying out the provisions of the Bill. As the rules will relate to matter of detail only, the delegation of legislative power is of normal character.

21

LOK SABHA

A

BILL

to provide for the establishment of an effective system to protect refugees and asylum-seekers by means of an appropriate legal framework to determine claims for asylum and to provide for the rights and obligations flowing from such status and matters connected therewith.

(Dr. Shashi Tharoor, M.P.)

GMGIPMRND—3088LS(S3)—10-12-2015.